Living, Leisure and Law

Eight Building Types in England 1800-1914

Living, Leisure and Law

Eight Building Types in England 1800–1914

Edited by Geoff Brandwood

Spire Books Ltd

PO Box 2336, Reading RG4 5WJ
www.spirebooks.com

Published in association with the Victorian Society

THE VICTORIAN SOCIETY

Spire Books Ltd
PO Box 2336
Reading RG4 5WJ
www.spirebooks.com

Copyright © 2010
Spire Books Ltd,
Geoff Brandwood
and the authors

CIP data:
A catalogue record for this book is available
from the British Library
ISBN 978-1-904965-27-5

Designed and produced by John Elliott
Text set in Bembo

Cover
Front: The façade at the Victoria & Albert Museum by Aston Webb.
Rear: Boathouse at Fell Foot, Staveley-in-Cartmel, Cumbria.

CONTENTS

Introduction

GEOFF BRANDWOOD

The years covered by this book – from the start of the nineteenth century down to the First World War – saw the arrival of an unprecedented number of new building types in Britain, and substantial changes of existing ones. The underlying reason is simple and obvious. The population, which stood at just over 8 million in 1801, rose to five times that figure by 1911, while GDP per capita roughly tripled over the same period. Such growth, unknown in human history, was founded on the achievements of the Industrial Revolution in a country with well-developed and stable financial and political institutions. Britain thus became covered with huge factories, ambitious country houses for the elite, railway stations, huge mass housing developments, buildings to facilitate commerce, and fine churches for the spiritual welfare of the booming population. Such are the great building types of the age, most of which have been extensively studied. But there are many others, less spectacular and less prominent, which were called into being or were transformed in this extraordinary age. Some have never been dealt with in print before.

To help bring such building types out of the shadows I organised a series of seven lectures for the Victorian Society in October and November 2009 under the (deliberately) slightly salacious title, 'Pleasure, Punishment and Protection'. They were given over consecutive weeks in the lecture hall at the Art Workers' Guild in London. It had proved an agreeably easy task to put the series together as there was no shortage of potential speakers. This clearly demonstrated that a great deal of work had been, and was being done on many of Britain's less well-known Victorian building types. Most of the participants were employees of, or had undertaken research for English Heritage. For various good reasons not all the lectures have been transformed into chapters for this book but it has been possible to include four studies (Temperance buildings, ferneries, museums, and post offices) not covered in the lectures. The building types covered here are a gloriously eclectic mix but they all have their fascination in different ways. This sheer diversity means there is no grand logic to the ordering, and the chapters may be read in any order as they take the reader's fancy.

In the first study Andrew Davison deals with the buildings of a quintessentially Victorian movement – Temperance. This crusade was pursued with quasi-religious fervour by its advocates who provided new buildings or reused others in order to promote their cause. The rise of Temperance was contemporaneous with another, but utterly different Victorian passion – ferns. Sarah Whittingham explains how the craze for ferns and ferneries made them an essential part of the well-appointed Victorian home and centrepieces in places of public enjoyment and institutions. Temperance and the fern craze are largely things of the past. Not so boathouses whose history stretches back to mid-Georgian times and which are still very much with us today. Adam Menuge discusses these little-known buildings and their importance to the elite who lived and played in the Lake District.

A modest but highly specialised type of building which simply could not exist before the very end of Victoria's reign was the motor house. John Minnis explains the form they took and shows how essential they were to those wealthy enough to own the new beast that was starting to colonise our roads. Also new in the late Victorian period was purpose-built accommodation for the increasing numbers of women who found employment in our great cities, and Emily Gee explains how such provision was made in London.

Museums and galleries have a long history but, as Barbara Lasic shows, the golden age of their development was the nineteenth century, and this produced the grandest and largest buildings dealt with in this book. The enforcement of law has been an ever-present human concern, of course, but urban growth in the nineteenth century posed unprecedented challenges. These led, as Susie Barson reveals, to the provision of hundreds of police stations and court houses throughout our capital city, many of which have made distinctive contributions to the streetscape. The development of the postal service was one of the greatest, if not most immediately obvious, of Victorian communication achievements. Its vast expansion after the introduction of the Penny Post in 1840 led, as Robert Hradsky shows, to thousands of purpose-built (and often good) buildings across the length and breadth of Britain.

The Victorian Society's lecture series was partly funded by English Heritage, and this book has been made possible by its Historic Environment Enabling Programme. I, the speakers and authors, the Victorian Society, and Spire Books are deeply grateful for their support.

1 'Worthy of the Cause': The Buildings of the Temperance Movement

ANDREW DAVISON

Our town centres are increasingly dominated by hangar-like bars aimed at the young, supermarkets sell strong lager as a loss-leader to attract customers, and there is a rising chorus of concern about the long-term effects of excessive drinking, but no-one is suggesting the complete abolition of the liquor trade. Yet for over a century from 1830 the control or suppression of the liquor trade was a major political issue. It split the country, brought vast numbers of people onto the streets in demonstrations and counter-demonstrations, and influenced the outcome of more than one general election. The Temperance movement has virtually disappeared, its credibility destroyed by the example of the United States, where the introduction of Prohibition in 1919 served only to hand control of the liquor trade to organised crime. Social historians have studied the rise and fall of the Temperance movement in considerable detail; rather less attention has been paid to the movement's buildings.

THE ORIGINS OF THE TEMPERANCE MOVEMENT

Alcohol was all-pervasive in early nineteenth-century England. Water was often polluted, and milk unsafe to drink, with the result that beer was drunk almost universally as refreshment and as an accompaniment to meals, as it had been for centuries. The introduction of stronger drinks, such as gin, during the eighteenth century, led to a steady increase in the number of outlets for alcohol, with social consequences which caused increasing concern to the respectable classes. Attempts by the Government to control the sale and consumption of alcohol were ineffectual. Eighteenth-century attempts to control the gin trade had little effect, whilst the Beer Act of 1830, intended to encourage the drinking of wholesome British beer at the expense of fancy foreign spirits, caused an explosion in the number of drinking establishments whilst reducing official control over them.[1] The circumstances were ripe for the emergence of the Temperance movement.

Temperance as a concept emerged in the United States where the first societies appeared in the 1820s, but it soon crossed the Atlantic. Temperance societies were founded in Belfast, Dublin and Glasgow during 1829, and the first one in England was set up in Bradford in February 1830. Others soon followed in Warrington (April), Manchester (May), Liverpool (July), Bristol (October) and London (November), the movement spreading until, by the end of June 1831, there were thirty such societies in England. These early societies endorsed the drinking of beer and wine in moderation, but were totally opposed to the consumption of spirits. They drew much of their support from the middle and upper classes, as well as from the established Church, and their endorsement of beer-drinking meant that brewers were often enthusiastic supporters. However, the character of the movement changed significantly during the 1830s, following the adoption of the 'total abstinence' or 'teetotal' pledge by the Preston Temperance Society on 1 September 1832. Other societies followed Preston's lead, and by 1840 the 'moderation' Temperance movement was effectively dead. Temperance lost many of its middle-class supporters as a result, and took on a distinctly lower-class and Nonconformist character.

THE NEED FOR BUILDINGS

The move to total abstinence created many problems for the movement, not least a need for accommodation. England in the 1830s had relatively few public halls or assembly rooms, except in the larger towns. Most public meetings and social gatherings were held in inns and public houses, and much of the country's social life revolved around these facilities and the drink available in them. By taking the revolutionary step of rejecting alcohol, the Temperance movement effectively debarred itself from using these premises. In some towns public halls might be available, although in many cases these were only really suitable for larger gatherings to mark special occasions, like the meeting to mark the third anniversary of Norwich's 'Teetotalist Society' at the Corporation-owned St Andrew's Hall on 2 October 1839.[2] Otherwise, facilities might be made available in sympathetic chapels or their school-rooms, but the general lack of accommodation placed additional pressure on a campaign whose supporters already faced considerable hostility due to their rejection of alcohol. The newspapers and broadsheets produced in large numbers to publicise the work of the movement contain many accounts of successful meetings, and the signing up of new supporters in their thousands, but they also tell of meetings broken up by angry mobs, and Temperance campaigners set upon by thugs in the pay of brewers or publicans. The *Preston Temperance Advocate* for August 1835, for example, reported that in Chester, 'the Mayor, a decided friend to the Temperance Society, had kindly lent out the Town Hall, but owing to repeated outrages….has withdrawn the use of it for the present'.

The Temperance movement needed to provide its own accommodation for meetings, for education, and for refreshment, if it was to resist pressure upon its members and support them in their struggle against the demon drink. The movement's aspirations were summarised by the committee of the Manchester and Salford Temperance Society in the *Star of Temperance* for September 1835. They were 'sensible of the importance of not only persuading the drunkard to leave those dangerous places of resort, the public-houses and beer and gin shops, but the imperative necessity of providing them with suitable and innocent places of amusement as substitutes'. They hoped to achieve this by 'establishing in various parts of the town coffee-houses and eating-houses … opening reading-rooms, either separately or in conjunction with coffee-houses, supplied with generally useful books … endeavouring to form … writing and reading schools … the delivery of monthly or weekly lectures on important subjects connected with the interests of the working classes, in addition to meetings held on behalf of temperance … [and] establishing friendly societies or sick clubs … in private rooms and not in public-houses'.

It seemed to many in the movement that these aspirations could only be realised by acquiring premises of their own. The opening of a Temperance hall at Garstang, Lancashire, on 24 November 1834 was the result of the first of many campaigns to do so. The Garstang hall was a simple wooden hut erected by voluntary labour, following objections from some members of the Methodist and Independent chapels in the town to the use of their buildings for Temperance meetings. Despite 'being only labouring men', the members of the Garstang Temperance Society raised funds from sympathisers in the town and in the surrounding area, located and purchased land, and erected their hall, all within a matter of a few months. In an exercise in branding which would not disgrace a modern advertising agency, the nearby Preston Temperance Society christened it 'The Lighthouse'.

Inspired by Garstang's example, other Temperance societies began to raise funds to obtain their own facilities. 'If we had had accommodation on neutral ground, for 1000 people, I believe they would have been present. We have again agitated for a large public building, and shares amounting to £600 are available through humble individuals', wrote a Darlington correspondent to the *Preston Temperance Advocate* in April 1835.

The second Temperance hall in England, which opened at Burnley on Christmas Eve, 1837, was a conversion of an earlier building which had been purchased by the local society. Conversion of existing premises offered the quickest and most effective route for any Temperance group seeking a base. Former chapels, meeting-houses and school-rooms were preferred, since they needed little alteration to render them suitable for Temperance meetings, lectures and other activities, but buildings with more unusual origins were also the Temperance Hall, a large and handsome building, of Doric architecture, erected in 1840 at the sole expense of R.D. Alexander, Esq', according to White's *History, Gazetteer, and Directory of Suffolk* for 1844. 'This Hall', it added, 'will accommodate 800 persons, being 68 feet long, and 40½ wide, and having a spacious gallery and platform'. 'The style of architecture is of the Grecian order', reported the *British Temperance Advocate & Journal* for 15 January 1840 of the Temperance hall, Bolton (**Fig. 2**), 'a noble building, situate in St George's Road' which had been opened on New Year's Day, and 'great pains have been taken to make it at once worthy of the cause and an ornament to the town'. Built at a cost of £2,200, it was said to hold almost 7,000 people.

Like other early examples, the interior of the Bolton Temperance Hall was reminiscent of a chapel, with a long gallery along its south wall, and a smaller one on the north, which was reserved for lecturers or an orchestra (**Fig. 3**). 'The walls of the interior are worked in imitation of stone, and the ceiling of plaster of Paris, with an ornamental cornice, and circle of moulded work in the centre. It will be brilliantly lighted with gas from four chandeliers of bronze, each chandelier having six branches'. Where the Temperance hall differed from the typical chapel was in the arrangements for making and serving tea. The Bolton hall could provide tea for up to 900 people at a time, and was fitted out with 'apparatus for boiling the water … on an enlarged and improved scale'. The two boilers held 50 gallons of water each, and would boil within twenty minutes; the *British Temperance Advocate* thought it particularly noteworthy that the water was supplied direct from the Bolton water-works. Providing tea for such numbers called for some ingenious furniture: 'some of the forms are so constructed that they can be made into tables, by drawing them up from the stand, and turning down a leaf on each side'.

Whilst the Nonconformist chapel provided the model for the majority of Temperance halls, not all followed the classical template. The Chesham Temperance Hall, built in 1852, is more reminiscent of the simple Nonconformist meeting houses of the late seventeenth century, whilst many halls in more rural areas were little more than simple huts.

THE MOVEMENT DEVELOPS

Like many popular movements, after an initial surge in enthusiasm and support, the Temperance movement had to weather a period when support dwindled as a result of the failure to achieve its objectives. No doubt some of the disillusionment was due to the discovery that many societies now found themselves saddled with buildings which were expensive to maintain, whilst fund-raising to acquire them in the first place had distracted attention from what many saw as the core activity of reclaiming drunkards. Not all activists were convinced that dedicated facilities were necessary, and the balance

Fig. 3 The spacious interior of the Bolton Temperance Hall, as depicted in the *Illustrated London News,* 2 October 1852. One of the galleries, normally used by lecturers or musicians accompanying the singing of campaigning songs, can be clearly seen.

between buildings and campaigning remained a subject of debate for decades. Joseph Livesey of Preston, the 'Father of Temperance', expressed a widely held view in the *Staunch Teetotaller* for May 1867. In reply to an MP who had claimed that temperance buildings needed to be of superior quality in order to fight the public houses on equal terms, he argued that 'The temperance people have not the cash to begin with, and to do as he suggested means getting into debt and difficulties'. Livesey preferred to see temperance activists working among the people – 'We must attack the drink traffic with something more effectual than paint, plate glass, and gilding'.

The movement began to revive in the late 1840s. A key event was the foundation of the Band of Hope in 1847. It concentrated on the young, with considerable success; by 1889 it had over two million members, a quarter of the population under 16. A second key event was the passing in June 1851, by the state of Maine in the United States, of the first law outlawing the sale of alcohol altogether. Inspired by this, the Temperance movement discovered a new appetite for campaigning, with the new aim of eradicating the alcohol trade altogether. The United Kingdom Alliance for the Suppression of the Traffic in all Intoxicating Liquors, which was founded in 1853 specifically to lobby for prohibition, had eventually to modify its aims in the light of significant opposition from its working-class audience, and it adopted a policy of 'local option' under which decisions on whether licenses should be issued would be taken by regular local referenda. The established Church, whose mission to relieve poverty in poor urban areas brought it increasingly into contact with the effects of alcohol abuse, renewed its commitment to Temperance by setting up the Church of England Temperance Society in 1861. It grew into the largest adult Temperance group in the country, with nearly 200,000 members by the end of the century. A further wave of enthusiasm towards the end of the 1870s saw the foundation of the Blue Ribbon Association, inspired by an American movement of the same name, which used showmanship and carefully staged events to drive home the Temperance message. The Salvation Army, founded in 1878 by William and Catherine Booth, was organised on military lines. Like the Church of England Temperance Society, it concentrated its efforts on relieving the suffering of the urban poor, with a network of local groups, managed by paid officers and staffed by volunteers.

LATER TEMPERANCE HALLS

The growth of the Temperance movement during the second half of the nineteenth century was reflected in the number of halls built across the country, until by 1900 virtually every town could boast at least one, and many larger centres had several. In areas where the movement was particularly strong many villages also had a Temperance hall. Whilst early Temperance halls tended to follow the classical model of the contemporary Nonconformist chapel, those built later in the nineteenth century were much more varied. Some had few pretensions. The West End Temperance Hall, Carlisle, of 1861; the Temperance Hall and Mechanics' Institute of 1866-7 at Armley, Leeds; the Temperance Hall of 1868 at Epworth in North Lincolnshire (**Fig. 4**); the tiny rendered hall of 1872 at Ireleth, Cumbria; and the corrugated iron sectional building which served as the hall at Hexham, Northumberland, are typical of the plain and simple buildings which sufficed for many Temperance

Fig. 4 The Epworth Temperance Hall of 1868, a simple brick-built structure with little in the way of architectural embellishment, was typical of many rural Temperance Halls. [Author].

Fig. 5 Simple sectional buildings in timber or corrugated iron provided accommodation for many Temperance societies. In a late nineteenth-century photograph, the Temperance Band line up proudly outside the wooden Temperance Hall in Walsham-le-Willows, Suffolk. According to the *Walsham Village History Group Quarterly Review*, no. 10, July 1999, both hall and band were founded by a local builder, Mr Nunn, who had been moved to embrace Temperance on a visit to London. [Author's collection].

societies (**Fig. 5**). Others adopted the Gothic style which was increasingly employed for respectable public and religious buildings. One of the earliest was the Cirencester Temperance Hall, Thomas Street, built at the expense of Christopher Bowly in 1846; but many others survive, such as the Newbury Temperance Hall, Northcroft Lane (1859); the Temperance Hall of 1868 at Finedon, Northamptonshire (**Fig. 6**); that of 1876 in Ward Street, Guildford; that of 1884 at Roche, Cornwall; and that of 1891 in Cross Street, Cromer, Norfolk (these last two in a very simplified Gothic style indeed). Yet others employed more eclectic styles, incorporating mixtures of Renaissance and other elements, as in the Temperance halls of 1873 at Banbury, and of 1876 at Halstead, Essex, both of which incorporated branches of the 'British Workman' teetotal public-house chain, and that of 1895 at Morley, West Yorkshire. Most Temperance halls bore a simple inscription stating their purpose, but some took the opportunity to broadcast the Temperance message; the façade of the Worcester Temperance Hall, built in the 1860s in polychrome brick (demolished in 1900), incorporated a band between the ground and first floor,

Fig. 6 The Temperance Hall of 1868 at Finedon, Northamptonshire (now the Town Hall) emphasises the respectability of the Temperance cause through use of the Gothic style. [Author].

which bore in relief the slogan 'The blessing of God keep us and protect us from all intoxicating drinks'.[7]

From the earliest days of the movement, Temperance halls had incorporated libraries, news-rooms and school-rooms. Some had included facilities which might generate income to sustain the hall whilst spreading the Temperance gospel, hence the hotel incorporated in the Pocklington Temperance Hall, and the teetotal public houses included in the Banbury and Halstead halls. St James's Hall, New York Street, Leeds, designed by Thomas Ambler in 1877 in Gothic Revival style, was part of a complex which included coffee, dining, reading and smoking rooms on the ground floor, club rooms and the manager's apartment on the second floor, and dormitory apartments for travellers and working men on the third floor in addition to the first-floor hall itself. A modest mid-Victorian hall at Keighley, West Yorkshire, was replaced in 1896 by a much more impressive Temperance Hall and Institute, designed by W. and J.B. Bailey in Baroque style, which incorporated a number of shop units to provide rental income (**Fig. 7**).

The Temperance halls of the later nineteenth century were often to be found in the better parts of town, reflecting the respectable image of the movement. The Salvation Army, by contrast, was dedicated to its mission amongst the urban poor. Its halls, (referred to as 'citadels' in keeping with its military ethos) were built in the areas where their clients lived – areas of slums and sub-standard housing, from which the public house offered the only appealing escape. The military parallels, and the Salvationists' view of themselves as working for good whilst surrounded by the forces of evil, were reflected in citadel design. They were typically fortress-like in appearance, as surviving examples in towns like Hexham, dating from 1883 (**Fig. 8**), Barrow-in-Furness, Cumbria, of 1910, and Harwich, Essex, demonstrate. As one of the few organisations dedicated to Temperance to have survived into the twenty-first century, the Salvation Army continues to erect new buildings.

THE TWENTIETH CENTURY

The Temperance movement was at its strongest in the first decade of the twentieth century. Responding to Temperance pressure, new Licensing Acts in 1902 and 1904 gave magistrates wide-ranging powers to control licensed houses, and instituted a scheme for reducing their numbers, financed by a levy on owners. Agitation for more far-reaching legislation was ultimately unsuccessful, however. The Liberal Government's Licensing Bill of 1908,

Fig. 7 The Temperance Hall & Institute of 1896 at Keighley, West Yorkshire. Replacing an earlier Temperance Hall, it included a range of facilities. [Author].

Fig. 8 The Salvation Army Citadel in Market Street, Hexham, is dated 1883, only five years after the organisation's foundation. It appears to be a conversion of an earlier building, but the battlements were to be a standard feature of Salvation Army citadels for many years. [Author].

which proposed to reduce the number of licenses by a third over fourteen years, to introduce 'local option', and to ban the employment of women in pubs, brought matters to a head. The Temperance movement put millions of marchers on to the streets in support of the Bill, but counter-marches attracted almost as many, whilst there was widespread sympathy for barmaids, who formed the Barmaids' Political Defence League to fight for their jobs. The Bill was eventually defeated in the Lords, despite being passed by the Commons. Widespread celebrations at its fall suggested that the Temperance movement still had much work to do if alcohol was to be banished. The popularity of the movement began to wane soon afterwards; restrictions on the sale of alcohol imposed by the Government during the First World War proved widely unpopular, and the failure of Prohibition in the United States caused many to question the movement's credibility. By the outbreak of the Second World War Temperance was in serious decline.

Few Temperance halls were built in the twentieth century. Two rare surviving examples are Sydney Hall, Pond Place, SW3, built by the Chelsea Temperance Society in 1908 to replace a much earlier hall, and what may be the very last Temperance hall to be built in England, that of 1910 at Bainbridge in North Yorkshire, a simple building enlivened by touches of Art Nouveau decoration. However, most towns and villages with any Temperance activity had acquired the necessary facilities by the end of the previous century, and waning enthusiasm for Temperance before the First World War now led to increasing numbers of closures and disposals. Temperance halls were particularly suited to conversion to cinemas: Bolton's became the 'Temperance Hall Cinema' in 1908, and was rebuilt as the 'Rialto' in the 1920s, whilst Bridport's became the 'Electric Palace Cinema'. Closures accelerated after the First World War, with many Temperance halls in rural areas becoming village halls and community centres. More varied uses were found for redundant urban halls. The Chesham Temperance Hall became an amateur theatre, that at Leighton Buzzard became a public library, and the Derby Temperance Hall was sold to the local Conservative Association in 1946, becoming the 'Churchill Hall'.

TEMPERANCE HOTELS

Temperance halls provided a secure base from which the message could be spread, but other facilities were also necessary if converts were not to be seduced from their commitment to total abstinence. The only accommodation available to travellers in the England of the 1830s was in inns and public houses, which were also the most obvious places to find food and drink. For many early Temperance campaigners the difficulty in finding suitable accommodation when away from home was a more pressing concern than finding premises to house their meetings. The *Moral Reformer* for July 1832 echoed their concerns: 'We still lack one thing, the necessity of which we feel more and more every day, and that is a "Temperance House" … [where] persons would be supplied with good water, milk, tea, coffee, or any sort of harmless beverage, and meet with all the accommodations of a respectable eating house … and if beds and stables were kept for travellers, these houses would be complete establishments for temperate persons'. The opportunity offered by this growing demand did not escape entrepreneurs, and the opening of the first Temperance hotel, on Church Street in Preston, on Christmas Eve 1832, was followed very shortly afterwards by the opening of hotels in Bolton, Huddersfield, Manchester and Oldham. The *Preston Temperance Advocate* for January 1834 commented:

> Temperance Houses, called by different names, have been attempted in several towns in Lancashire. Of their utility there can be no doubt, and it is vain ever to expect Temperance to prevail without houses of this sort … whether they be called simply Temperance House or Temperance Coffee House, or Temperance Hotel, they should have something in their designation to indicate that they are *eating houses*….and perhaps Victualling House is as appropriate as any other … Four *objects* which should be sought to be accomplished … [are] a respectable *eating* house … a respectable *lodging* house, to accommodate persons who object to stopping at public houses … a place of casual accommodation, where persons can come to transact business, read the papers, or enjoy social intercourse, or where parties, societies and committees can meet for similar purposes. The above are the most important objects, but rather than let people go to the public-houses…it is also recommended to supply various liquids which are pleasant to the taste … coffee, tea, milk, ginger beer, lemonade, peppermint water and raspberry vinegar. The latter are much in use, diluted with hot water, and sweetened.

Fig. 9 The former Drayton's Temperance Hotel, West Street, Crewkerne, Somerset, typical of many small-town Temperance hotels, is probably a conversion of a rather earlier building. [Author].

The *Preston Temperance Advocate* for November 1835 listed 22 Temperance hotels spread across northern and midland England from Newcastle in the north to Birmingham in the south, and Leeds in the east to Knutsford in the west. Not all of these 'hotels' provided overnight accommodation – some provided only food and drink, plus usually a news or reading room stocked with Temperance publications – but most, like the Commercial Coffee House in Oldham Street, Manchester, which opened in late 1833, provided beds for travellers. This establishment proved so popular that its proprietor, Sarah Brown, was able to move to larger premises only a year later.[8]

Temperance hotels soon began to spread beyond the original northern and midland heartlands of the movement. In April 1836 the British Tee-total Temperance Coffee-Rooms and Hotel, at 159 Aldersgate Street, became the first establishment to open in London, conveniently located for those with business in the City. Larger towns began to offer a choice of accommodation for the traveller who preferred to avoid alcohol. Bristol, for example, offered a choice between the Temperance Hotel and Commercial House at 17, Narrow Wine Street, opened in late 1835, and the Bristol Temperance Hotel, on the corner of Bath Street and Thomas Street, opened in December 1836, which, unusually, was operated by the Bristol Tee-total Temperance Society rather than by a private individual.[9]

By 1850 the teetotal traveller need not fear the temptation of alcohol, but could stay at a Temperance hotel in almost any town in the country. Not all offered their guests a comfortable experience; many hotels, particularly in the early years of the movement, were owned and operated by people who were mainly motivated by the opportunity to make money, and there were recurring complaints in the Temperance newspapers about the quality of the accommodation offered. Most early hotels were, in any case, conversions or re-fittings of existing premises which had been built for other purposes, and the accommodation was often cramped and spartan as a result (**Fig. 9**).

Firms dedicated to providing a better experience for the teetotal traveller began to appear in the 1870s. The Temperance Hotels Company Ltd was founded in 1872 to provide quality hotels in larger towns, whilst Trevelyan Temperance Hotels offered superior accommodation in London, Leeds and Manchester, in buildings specifically built for the purpose. Leeds, in particular, has several surviving buildings which were purpose-built as Temperance hotels, including the former Trevelyan Temperance Hotel of 1872 on the corner of Boar Lane and Briggate, an impressive building in Second Empire style by the fashionable local architect Thomas Ambler (**Fig. 10**). The hotel forming part of the St James's Hall complex in New York Street was aimed at the more cost-conscious traveller, with accommodation in dormitories rather than in individual rooms. Built in 1877, its instant popularity lead to its enlargement in 1884. Yet the only characteristic which actually distinguished Temperance hotels from their contemporaries was the lack of facilities for selling alcohol. 'Here is a house precisely like an inn, in every beneficial purpose … [but with] a total absence of wines and spirits', advertised the proprietor of the Temperance and Commercial Boarding House, Pilgrim-Street, Newcastle upon Tyne, in

Fig. 10 The Trevelyan Hotel of 1872, on the corner of Boar Lane and Briggate, in the centre of Leeds, was one of the most impressive Temperance hotels in the country. [Author].

the *Preston Temperance Advocate* for March 1835. An undated late nineteenth-century plan of the Commercial Hotel, Newport Street in Bolton,[10] shows an imposing three-storey building, with a total of 22 bedrooms divided between the first and second floors, and the ground floor occupied by a commercial room, smoke room, kitchen, scullery, room for storing luggage, lavatories and a shop. The basement incorporated a 'wash cellar', drying room and billiard room. Only a bar is missing.

THE COFFEE-HOUSE MOVEMENT
Whether dignified with the title 'hotel' or not, coffee-houses and eating-houses were key elements of the Temperance campaign from the beginning. As well as offering tea, coffee, cold drinks and food, many also featured news-rooms or reading-rooms, with a selection of newspapers, journals, Temperance tracts and other improving reading matter; some also offered rooms for meetings. They were intended to spread the Temperance message to those attracted by their cheap, good-value food and drink, but made no attempt to replicate the appearance or atmosphere of the public house.

There was a change in tactics in the 1850s, with the appearance of 'public

Fig. 11 The Ossington Coffee Palace, Newark-on-Trent, of 1882, was one of the largest and most impressive of all coffee taverns. Despite aristocratic patronage, and a wide range of facilities, it was not a commercial success. [Author].

houses', not dissimilar to the beerhouses of the day, selling coffee and snacks rather than alcohol. The first appeared in Dundee in 1853, and within a decade similar establishments had appeared in Manchester and London. In September 1867 the first 'British Workman's Public House' opened in Leeds. This was deliberately designed to look like a pub, and to provide a similar ambience, but instead of alcohol provided a range of temperance drinks, as well as coffee and food. It was a success, and further British Workman's houses opened around the country over the next few years. The formula was rapidly taken up by others, and some campaigners sought to get their message across by purchasing actual public houses and converting them to Temperance houses. In October 1872, for example, the social reformer Dr Barnardo bought the Edinburgh Castle, Limehouse, and re-opened it in 1873 as the Edinburgh Castle Coffee Palace; a second pub, the Dublin Castle, in Mile End Road, followed in 1875.[11]

A number of companies were founded to operate Temperance pubs. One of the largest was the Liverpool British Workman Public House Company, founded in March 1875 with a capital of £20,000. Within a year the company was operating five houses in the city, and by 1892 there were over 90 in Liverpool and the surrounding area, the company paying a healthy dividend on shares for some years.[12] A trade association, the Coffee Public House Association, was founded in 1877, and provided loans for those wishing to start up new businesses, among other services.

Some coffee pubs were, like the Edinburgh Castle and the Dublin Castle, former public houses which had been converted to the Temperance cause, but many more were purpose-built, and designed to look like pubs, with all the cut glass, mirrors and lamps of the late Victorian 'gin-palace'. The Cobden Coffee House, in Corporation Street, Birmingham, opened by the Birmingham Coffee-House Company in 1883 (now demolished), was arguably the most magnificent of all. An enormous Gothic building, it was designed by William Doubleday to outshine the most splendid pubs the city could offer, with stained and diamond-cut glass and spectacular tilework.[13]

Others avoided such vulgarity, being designed in restrained architectural styles which were to influence the 'improved' public houses of the early twentieth century. The Cowper Arms, in Cheapside, Luton, designed by Charles Bell for the Bedfordshire Coffee Tavern Company, is built in 'olde English' style, its brick and rendered frontage reminiscent of the work of Norman Shaw. The plans of the Cowper Arms, published in *The Builder* for 14 October 1882, show how closely the building resembled the better contemporary public houses, with two bars and a dining room on the ground floor, and ladies' room, smoking room and billiard room above, although it is unlikely that many pub owners of the period would have provided a 'chess room'.

Coffee pubs were also sponsored by the well-to-do. The Bee-Hive, Streatham (1879), designed by Ernest George in the 'Queen Anne' style, was built for local businessman P.B. Cow, the manufacturer of 'Cow Gum'. George also designed the Ossington Coffee Palace, Newark-on-Trent (1882), described on its dedication plaque as 'a perfect model of a 17th cent. hostelry' (**Fig. 11**). Built on the instructions of Viscountess Ossington in memory of her husband and nephew, it is very deliberately 'olde English' in style. It cost the enormous sum of £20,000, and contained bars, an assembly room, reading room, club room and billiard room, as well as letting bedrooms, whilst behind it was stabling for 50 horses and a garden containing an American bowling alley.[14]

Although the Ossington Coffee Palace was an unusually large and elaborate example, it was typical of the coffee public house in several ways. It owed its existence to aristocratic sponsorship, and it was ultimately a commercial failure, although it was still in use as a Temperance hotel in 1910. A significant number of coffee pubs were built for local aristocrats or middle-class committees, and only survived whilst their sponsors were prepared to subsidise them. Few of these businesses seem to have been profitable; the attempt to replicate the public house experience was difficult without the social lubrication of alcohol, and many of the managers running them were

Fig. 12 The High Cross, Leicester, of 1895, was designed by Edward Burgess for the Leicester Coffee & Cocoa House Company. It was a popular venue with the Leicester public, perhaps because no attempt was made to ape a public house. By a twist of fate, it is now a Wetherspoon's pub. [Author].

selected because of their commitment to Temperance rather than because of their business ability. Above all, the tendency of the Temperance movement to preach alienated potential customers. Where coffee pubs were operated by commercial companies on strict business lines, they were very much more successful.

The Temperance cafés, coffee-houses and cocoa-houses which began to appear alongside the coffee public houses in the later 1870s provided non-alcoholic refreshments, food and entertainment in buildings which made no pretence at being public houses, and enjoyed increasing success as a result. Although they had their roots in the earlier Temperance coffee-houses, they were also influenced by continental models. The Leicester Coffee & Cocoa House Company, for example, was founded in July 1877 with the object of establishing 'houses, rooms, coffee carts, stalls and other places' in and around Leicester to provide non–alcoholic refreshment. With the exception of the first of the company's houses, the Granby, which was a conversion of an existing building, the majority of the company's estate was purpose-built, designed by the local architect Edward Burgess, who used a variety of architectural styles. The High Cross (1895), on High Street, is built of red brick with white masonry dressings and decoration (**Fig. 12**), whilst the East Gates (1885), on the corner of Church Gate opposite the Clock Tower, is 'in the domestic style of the fifteenth century'. The most impressive of the Leicester coffee-houses, the Victoria (1888) in Granby Street, was designed 'in the style of the French Renaissance'.[15]

The Leicester company's establishments were very popular, and known for the range of their facilities as well as the quality and value of their food and drink. Trade began to decline in the first decade of the twentieth century, however, and the company went into liquidation in 1921 in the face of competition from more modern cafés and restaurants which began to spring up, not only in Leicester, but in every town in the country; many of them were designed, like those of the Leicester company, by very competent architects. The Worcester diocesan architect, Louis Sheppard, for example, was responsible for the design of the New Central Coffee Tavern in Worcester, an imposing example of contemporary commercial architecture opened in 1901.

TEMPERANCE RECREATION

Temperance campaigners lost no opportunity to demonstrate that activities popularly associated with drinking could also be enjoyed without it. There were even attempts to promote a Temperance version of the music hall, a highly popular form of working-class entertainment with its origins firmly in the mid nineteenth-century public house, and notorious for the alcohol-fuelled high spirits of its audience. The Colosseum Theatre, Paradise Street, Liverpool, was

Fig. 13 The Sedge Lynn public house, Chorlton-cum-Hardy, Manchester, of 1907, was originally designed for the Temperance Billiard Hall Company of Pendleton by their architect Norman Evans. The barrel vault, dormers, and green-glazed tiles are typical of the company's style. [Author].

opened as a Temperance music hall in late 1879, but was successful only until the novelty wore off after a few months. The Royal Victoria Coffee Tavern Music Hall in Lambeth, offering 'Variety Entertainments, after the style of the ordinary music halls, but free from any objectionable features', was similarly unsuccessful; it eventually evolved to become the Old Vic Theatre.[16]

Billiards became a popular pastime during the second half of the ninteenth century. It was initially closely identified with the public house, but towards the end of the century halls specifically dedicated to billiards began to appear. The earliest billiard halls served alcohol to their customers, but Temperance versions soon put in an appearance. The popularity of the game was reflected in the size of some of the establishments; a turn of the century plan of the Temperance Billiard Hall on the corner of Manchester Road and Bridgeman

Fig. 14 The former Temperance billiard hall on Fulham High Street, London, is now a public house. Designed in 1910 by Norman Evans, it is one of the Temperance Billiard Hall Company's more elaborate buildings, with two rectangular halls side by side.

Place, Bolton, shows a building housing 53 tables spread across four floors.[17]

Temperance Billiard Halls Ltd, founded in Manchester in 1906, became the largest promoter of these venues, building seventeen halls to the designs of their architect Norman Evans by 1911 (**Fig. 13**). The majority were in the suburbs of Manchester and nearby towns, but there were also a number in south London, at Balham, Clapham, Fulham, Lewisham and Wandsworth. The former Chorlton Snooker Centre in the Manchester suburb of Chorlton-cum-Hardy is typical of Evans' designs, featuring a long barrel-vaulted roof with dormers, exuberant Art Nouveau glass and tilework. It survived as a Temperance establishment until the 1990s, being converted to a public house by the Wetherspoon chain after closure. The best surviving London example, dating from 1910, is in Fulham High Street, and again features some spectacular tilework and stained glass (**Figs. 14, 15**). The hall at Bury, although no longer a Temperance establishment, survives in use as the Bury Snooker Centre. It is unusual in consisting of two barrel-vaulted halls side by side, and retains some of the decorative tilework which was a feature of Temperance Billiard Halls' premises.

Whilst Temperance Billiard Halls Ltd were the largest and best known promoters, they did not lack competition. Clegg's *Commercial Directory of Rochdale* for 1916 lists six public billiard halls in the town, in addition to six hotels where the game could be played. Three of the public halls were Temperance establishments, the Rochdale Temperance Billiard Hall on King Street having four tables and the Alexandra Temperance Billiard Hall on South

Fig. 15 An elegant bay window with Art Nouveau glass at the former Temperance billiard hall, Fulham High Street. [Geoff Brandwood].

Fig. 16 The Holme Head Coffee Tavern, Carlisle, with an adjacent reading-room, was built by local mill-owners Ferguson Bros for their workforce in 1881. Four years later, a bowling green was also provided. [Author].

Street eight, in addition to Temperance Billiards Halls Ltd's hall on Nelson Street, which had eighteen.

Temperance halls and institutes were normally built following fundraising by the campaigners themselves, whilst hotels, coffee taverns, cafés and billiard halls were usually operated as commercial concerns by entrepreneurs. Enlightened or paternalistic employers were also behind the provision of Temperance facilities. In 1860, for example, the Stockton & Darlington Railway Company (which clearly had an interest in ensuring that its employees were sober and alert) provided a building for its employees comprising a library, lecture room, reading room, committee, and classrooms, together with a refreshment room which served only coffee and soft drinks.[18]

Many other employers followed suit, providing their employees with accommodation or leisure facilities from which alcoholic drinks were banned. Facilities ranged from a single building, such as the coffee tavern and reading-room at Holme Head, Carlisle, built in 1881 to the designs of George Dale Oliver for local firm Ferguson Bros (**Fig. 16**), to a complete drink-free estate such as those at Saltaire (Bradford), built for Sir Titus Salt between 1850 and 1872, or Ackroydon (Halifax), founded by Colonel Edward Ackroyd in 1859. The mill-owning founders of Ackroydon and Saltaire had no personal objections to alcohol, but were well aware of its potential impact on productivity. Other model settlements were founded by employers who *did* have both moral and religious objections to alcohol, that at Bournville (Birmingham), largely dating from the period 1894-90, by the Cadbury family, and New Earswick (York), begun in 1901, by the Rowntrees. These model settlements directly influenced the 'garden village' and 'garden city' movements of the first half of the twentieth century.[19]

CONCLUSION

The Temperance movement had a major impact on political and social life for over a century, yet today it has almost completely vanished. Very few establishments now operate on explicitly Temperance principles – a bar in Rawtenstall, Lancashire, a pub at Cautley, Cumbria, and a few hotels operated by an arm of the Salvation Army are virtually the only examples. The visible legacy of the Temperance movement survives in a few buildings bearing the inscription 'Temperance Hall' or 'Temperance Institute', and others which now bear little sign of their original purpose, but once proudly flew the Temperance banner as hotels or coffee pubs. Space precludes mention of anything other than the main types of Temperance building. There is no mention, for example, of more esoteric buildings such as the London Temperance Hospital in Hampstead Road, opened in 1881, at a time when alcohol featured in many medical treatments and brewers proudly advertised the health-giving qualities of their product. Nor is there any mention of the statues, drinking fountains and water-troughs which were sponsored by Temperance campaigners to celebrate the heroes of the movement or to emphasise the value of water as refreshment. Yet today public houses are closing at an alarming rate, and our town centres are populated with coffee shops in a way which would not have seemed credible to even the most ardent 'Teetotalist' of the 1830s. Perhaps the legacy of the Temperance movement is greater than might be imagined.

Notes

1. The Act allowed any ratepayer to sell beer after payment of an annual Excise fee of two guineas. A licence from the Justices of the Peace, who had been responsible for regulation since 1495, was no longer required. Beer duty was abolished although that on the raw materials of malt and hops remained. The only restriction was that the new beerhouses had to close between 10pm and 4am on weekdays and could only open on Sundays between 1 and 3pm and 5 to 10pm. Public houses (which sold other types of alcohol) had only to close during Sunday morning church services.
2. Charles Mackie, 'Norfolk Annals', vol. 1, Norwich: *Norfolk Chronicle*, 1901, p. 388.
3. *British Temperance Advocate & Journal*, 24 October 1840, p. 123.
4. P. T. Winskill, *The Temperance Movement and its Workers*, vol. 1, London, 1892, p. 183.
5. Ibid., vol. 2, pp. 113, 117.

6. *British Temperance Advocate & Journal*, 15 November 1839, p. 128.

7. www.worcesterpeopleandplaces.com.

8. *Preston Temperance Advocate*, January 1834, p. 16; January 1835, p. 8.

9. Ibid., April 1836, p. 32; January 1836, p. 8; December 1836, p. 96.

10. Bolton Archives, JBO/9/337.

11. Mark Girouard, 'Pubs with no Beer', *Country Life*, 9 October 1975, p. 926.

12. P.T. Winskill & J. Thomas, *The History of the Temperance Movement in Liverpool and District,* Liverpool, 1887, p. 76.

13. Girouard, 'Pubs with no Beer', p. 928.

14. Mark Girouard, *Victorian Pubs*, New Haven & London, 1984 (reprint of 1975 edition), p. 204.

15. Malcolm Elliott, 'The Leicester Coffee-House and Cocoa-House Movement', *Transactions of the Leicestershire Archaeological & Historical Society*, 47, 1971-2, p. 58.

16. Winskill & Thomas, *The History of the Temperance Movement in Liverpool*, p. xxxi; Girouard, 'Pubs with no Beer', p. 926.

17. Bolton Archives, ABJ/19/14.

18. Winskill, *The Temperance Movement and its Workers*, vol. 2, p. 119.

19. Gillian Darley, *Villages of Vision*, London: Granada, 1978 (paperback reprint of 1975 edition), pp. 131-5, 139-40, 184-6.

2 'Ferns and Fountains and Fishpools; Crags and Caverns and Cascades': The Victorian Public Fernery

SARAH WHITTINGHAM

Of all the many passions and crazes in Victorian natural history and gardening, none was as long lasting, or as wide reaching, as 'Pteridomania', or fern fever.[1] From 1837 until World War I, hundreds of books and articles inspired botanists and gardeners to collect as many species and varieties of fern as they could. Those who did not care to trawl the countryside, or were unsuccessful in their searches, could buy plants from what were called Itinerant Fern Vendors or Professional Fern Touts. These characters scoured the hedgerows for specimens, sent them up to towns and cities by rail, and then sold them in the streets, or hawked them from door to door. Native and exotic ferns could also be obtained from many specialist nurseries.

Whether collected or bought, fern lovers' spoils were then either pressed and glued into albums and herbaria, or kept as a live collection in a fernery. This term was coined by the naturalist Edward Newman (1801-76), author of *A History of British Ferns* (1840) and *A History of British Ferns, and Allied Plants* (1844). In the late 1830s Newman began making walking tours of Wales, during which he became enamoured of ferns and started to grow and study them. He initially referred to his 'fern garden', but soon began using the name 'fernery' for his collection.[2] The word, partly though the influence of his books, passed into general usage, and subsequently came to be used to describe any one of three things: an indoor glass case, an outdoor area, or a glazed structure.

TYPES OF FERNERY

Although others had been experimenting with 'closely-glazed cases' to protect plants from the pollution of Victorian cities, it was Nathaniel Bagshaw Ward (1791-1868), who did the most to popularise them, after his discovery of the concept in 1829. Initially known as Ward's cases, Wardian cases full of ferns became ubiquitous in middle-class drawing rooms in the 1850s. This was after the onerous excise duty on glass was repealed in 1845, and the Great Exhibition of 1851, housed in the Crystal Palace in Hyde Park, made glass structures of all kinds extremely popular. A related feature was a glazed window case, either formed on the inside of a bay, or attached to the exterior of a sash window.

If pollution was not too much of a problem, native fern species could be grown outside. A hardy fernery could be made in a shady corner of a small garden or yard, but the ideal was a secluded spot some distance from the house, formed in a natural or man-made hollow. Often a rock garden and fern garden were assumed to be one and the same thing. This varied from little more than low mounds of rock, to rugged outcrops and caves, with water trickling or dripping on to mossy stones.

The classic fernery was a freestanding, glass-roofed structure that either had high stone or brick walls, or was semi-submerged, to provide the shade and dampness that native ferns require. Inside, the principal aim was to recreate a natural fern-clad ravine. The structure of the building was hidden as much as possible with rockwork and vegetation, and the planting was naturalistic in style. Although ferneries were often rectangular, authors recommended an L-shaped plan or irregular layout to add an element of surprise for the visitor. A meandering path, covered with tiles or pebble-mosaic, ran around the perimeter between rockwork covering the sides of the building and massed in the middle.

In the larger or more elaborate ferneries, the stone was built up into arches and 'ruins'. There could be alcoves, caves, grottoes, a subterranean passage, or stairways leading up to viewing platforms. Water was essential, and was usually

Section of a Fernery.

Fig. 1 A schematic section of a fernery from *The Garden*, 20 February 1875. The figure illustrated a private fernery recently constructed in Glasgow by Boyd & Sons. It has a very similar roof design to that of Benmore which was listed in the article as another one erected by the firm.

Fig. 2 The interior of the restored fernery at Benmore Botanic Garden. A natural rock face forms one wall (right), and is constantly dripping with water. On the middle level there is an arched, quartz-lined grotto, with a pool fed by a burn from above. [Author].

introduced in the form of a cascade down an end wall. It then flowed through the house in a series of pools crossed by a rustic bridge or two. The sound of water was important, and this was sometimes provided by way of a 'dropping' or 'dripping' well. As with Wardian cases, these features were introduced to provide a wide variety of growing conditions as well as for aesthetic reasons.

Private ferneries varied enormously in size, from small grottoes, through quite substantial structures in the gardens of the middle classes, to those on a scale rivalling public venues. Sometime between 1870 and 1875 James Duncan, a Greenock sugar refiner, employed James Boyd & Sons, horticultural builders of Paisley, to construct a fernery on his dramatic Scottish estate at Benmore, Argyllshire.[3] It was a huge – 1,532 square feet – rectangular, schist rubble-stone structure, with semi-circular gable ends and a glass roof. It was sited in a steep-sided rocky cleft some distance from the house. To a certain extent, it was a public space; Duncan was a keen art collector, and after showing visitors his paintings in a specially built gallery, would conduct them to the fernery to view his other collection, of ferns. (**Figs. 1, 2**).

Fig. 3. The east end of the Tropical Ravine House, Belfast Botanic Gardens. [Author].

FERNERIES FOR ALL

As well as being located in private homes and gardens, all three types of fernery could be found in locations open to all, and they shared many of the same characteristics and features. The Victorian middle classes believed in what was variously called rational recreation, entertainment, or amusement, both for themselves and the working classes. Free time was not to be frittered away in idleness, but spent pursuing edifying and educational activities. The study of natural history was a perfect way of satisfying this demand for continual improvement. Amateur naturalists occupied their time investigating the seashore, catching butterflies, tapping rocks with hammers, and setting out on fern forays.

In addition, natural history was an obsession among the middle and upper classes because it was believed that examining the 'Wonders of Creation' would 'Lead through Nature up to Nature's God.' Authors constantly avowed that there was no better group of plants to study than ferns in order to accomplish this. The nineteenth century was also the age of the plant collector, when thousands of new species were introduced to Britain. It is not surprising, therefore, that so many botanic gardens were founded in this period, and that they and their curators played a significant role in the fern craze. Botanic and zoological gardens provided the key combination of education and recreation, and a fernery was often one among many attractions on offer.

BOTANIC GARDENS

Birmingham Botanical Gardens opened in 1832, and by 1844 the collection of ferns numbered 360 species, including many rarities. In 1868 William Bradbury Latham was appointed curator, remaining there until 1903. He was an expert on the cultivation of orchids and exotic ferns, and the conservatory soon contained an important and much-praised collection of tree ferns. In addition, in the year that he arrived, Latham completed a 'Fern Walk' through an excavated sandstone hollow that had been begun six years earlier. This was planted with various hardy species, including *Osmunda regalis*, the royal fern.

Like many other botanic gardens, Birmingham had a special, humid, filmy fern house housing the rare Killarney fern, which was much sought after by Victorian collectors. Frederick Burbidge (1847-1905), curator of Trinity College Botanic Garden in Dublin, commented that there were probably more Killarney ferns growing in the Tropical Ravine House in Belfast than could be found in Killarney. He claimed that this fern house was one of the finest and most artistically arranged in Europe.[4] Also known as the Glen, the fernery was conceived by the curator, Charles McKimm (1848-1907), and constructed between 1887 and 1889. After Belfast Corporation bought the gardens from the Belfast Botanic and Horticultural Society in 1895 they

Fig. 4 Part of the temperate section of the Tropical Ravine House, Belfast Botanic Gardens. The pteridologist Charles Druery thought that the fernery gave 'a splendid idea of a tropical or subtropical glen, from the depths of which the larger vegetation springs, and towers up to a considerable height above the beholder's head.' (*Gardeners' Chronicle*, 17 December 1904). [Author].

remodelled the Glen at a cost of £1,000 in 1900. In 1902 they extended it to include a heated lily pond. The rectangular, two-storey, red-brick building was then 185 feet long and 45 feet wide, with a Dutch gable at the east end, and a glass gable at the west (**Fig. 3**).

The house was cut into a slope, and visitors came in at the upper, west end on to a narrow gallery that ran around the perimeter of the building about 12 feet above the ground. Unusually, as well as light coming down through the glass roof, the upper walls were lined with large, shallow-arched windows. Visitors looked down from the gallery into a glen, or ravine, of moss-covered red sandstone rocks, and through a lush tropical jungle of plants, including ferns, bananas, palms, bamboos and cycads, planted in raised, irregular beds, growing up the walls and in baskets hanging from the roof.

The 110-foot-long temperate section was entered first. In the 1900s 'specially conducted visitors' could descend rough stone steps to inspect more closely a small pool with a cascade operated by a pulley, and fight their way along winding paths through verdant foliage (**Fig. 4**). Doors on the ground and first floors led into the 75-foot-long stove section, with a rectilinear pool on the first floor on top of the boiler, built to house the giant South American water lily, *Victoria regia* (now *amazonica*). This section also had stone steps leading down into the undergrowth. The end wall, backing the pond, was originally covered with the *nephrolepis* genus of ferns, *Ficus repens* or creeping fig, and begonias.

The Southport & Churchtown Botanic Gardens & Museum Company was formed in 1874. Their 20-acre-gardens, including rockeries, fountains, grottoes and a boating lake, were laid out by John Shaw of Manchester and opened on 15 May 1875. In 1876 a huge conservatory, glazed fernery, museum and refreshment rooms, designed by architects Mellor & Sutton of Southport, were added. The fernery was hidden behind the conservatory and, externally, was fairly utilitarian in appearance: a low, rectangular building, about 120 feet long, with red brick walls and a plain glass roof. Inside, however, the walls were completely covered in artificial tufa up to the eaves and over the structural ironwork of the roof. Heating pipes were hidden in the rockwork. **(Fig. 5)**

At the north and south ends were grottoes with double flights of steps leading to viewing platforms on top. Mirrors on the walls behind the platforms, and along the sides of the house, reflected endless ferny vistas. Paths wound under 'tufa'-covered arches, and around pools and, if it were all too much, there were numerous seats. In the centre was a rustic, rocky fountain with a large basin constantly flowing with water. In 1875 *The British Architect* reported that the fernery would be 'fitted up in the best style with rock-work, and there will also be cascades, rivulets, and fountains, filled in with choice palms, tree ferns, mosses, &c.'[5] In a not entirely unbiased article, the *Southport Visitor* of 25

Fig. 5 Inside the 1876 fernery at Southport Botanic Gardens. The Southport Directory for 1894-5 described 'The Unique Fernery With its Fairy-like Foliage, Mirrors, Grottoes, Waterfalls, Fountain and Fishpools.' [Author].

January 1876 claimed that 'the fernery is fast assuming a beauty of outline and character, which already gives promise of its being, when completed, one of the loveliest ferneries in the kingdom.'

Many Victorians were obsessed with fairies and the fairy world, and ferneries were often described as a 'fairy grotto' or 'fairy land'. The *Southport Visitor* of 11 July 1876 thought that in the fernery '…"in cool grot and mossy cell," rural fairies ought to dwell, if they do not. But we fear if any of the pixies once know of this charming abode the directors will never get clear of them; they will be perpetual tenants.' Even *The British Architect* described the fernery as being 'divided into a series of fairy glens', and went on 'Art has almost eclipsed nature and the visitor may easily imagine he is in some enchanted ravine, where rippling water, splendid ferns, and fantastic rockeries charm the sight.'[6] In 1901 *Southport: Descriptive & Illustrative* summed it up as 'Ferns and fountains and fishpools; crags and caverns and cascades – it is indeed, a veritable fairy-land.'[7]

WINTER GARDENS

It is no coincidence that Southport Botanic Gardens and its myriad of attractions were at the seaside. Between 1870 and 1914 over 200 substantial entertainment buildings were constructed at resorts around the coast, in a never-ending struggle to woo the crowds. The holiday-maker was encouraged to feel removed from day-to-day life, and this was emphasised with oriental-style architecture and exotic, tropical plants. Two venues that not only always had ferns planted in them, but often contained a designated fernery as well, were winter gardens (part of the rise in popularity of all glass structures since the Great Exhibition) and aquaria. The fact that a fernery was considered a draw to the Victorian sightseer is indicative of the extent of Pteridomania.

The 1878 *Southport Directory* described the Botanic Gardens fernery as being 'unequalled in the North of England', but in 1889 an advertisement by the Blackpool Winter Gardens and Pavilion Company boasted that their Grand Fernery 'is acknowledged the finest ever constructed. It contains several superb specimens of Tree Ferns, 30 feet to 40 feet high; and the lovely Ferns and Waterfalls make this a perfect Paradise.'[8] The huge, glazed fernery was nearly 200 feet long, with a rockwork wall at one end, and sinuous paths winding around large mossy boulders, up steps and through arches (**Fig. 6**).

The vast and magnificent Blackpool Winter Gardens were designed by the architect Thomas Mitchell of Oldham, and opened in 1878. They comprised a collection of entertainment structures surrounding a theatre, including a glazed ambulatory, ornamental grounds, refreshment rooms and indoor and outdoor skating rinks. From 1897 the Victoria Street entrance was by way of the Floral Hall, which was 176 feet long, 44 feet wide and 25 feet high, and contained numerous magnificent palm trees and other exotics. In 1892 the

Fig. 6 The Grand Fernery, Blackpool Winter Gardens. The winter gardens and ferneries of the rich often included pieces of white marble sculpture to contrast with the dark green foliage. Blackpool appears to have possessed one, unusually mobile, statue that pops up in various positions in contemporary postcards. [Author's collection].

company was advertising a cornucopia of delights, including a 'Superb Floral Hall, Palm House, and Gigantic Fernery … Fairy Caves and Grottoes', with that irresistible combination of 'the very best of everything and cheap prices.'[9]

AQUARIA

Nathaniel Ward developed a version of his case, the vivarium, to house animals such as snakes, and the 'aqua vivarium', or aquarium, for fish. The religious naturalist Philip Henry Gosse (1810-88) believed that the beach provided the ideal place to study God's works, and did much to instigate and encourage the marine craze. In 1854 he published *The Aquarium: an Unveiling of the Wonders of the Deep Sea*, and the following year, *A Handbook to the Marine Aquarium: Containing Practical Instructions for Constructing, Stocking, and Maintaining a Tank, and for Collecting Plants and Animals*. The British coastline, particularly north Devon, was invaded by amateur naturalists peering into rock pools and capturing their contents.

In the mid-1850s no parlour was complete without a sea- or fresh-water aquarium. As Shirley Hibberd memorably wrote, 'Who would live contentedly, or consider a sitting-room furnished, without either a Ward's Case or an Aquarium?'[10] Some elaborate edifices even combined the two. However, home aquarium owners soon found that maintaining the right environment for their 'pets' was harder than it first appeared. Visiting a public aquarium run by 'experts' started to seem more appealing. These were usually very much in the style of grottoes: subterranean, atmospheric places, often with glazed roofs, that provided suitable conditions for growing ferns, which in their turn added to the green, underwater, ambience.

Very few aquaria were attractive enough to visitors in their own right to provide a sufficient income for their owners to cover the high costs of running them. Facilities on offer therefore included eating rooms, reading rooms, concert rooms and orchestras, roller-skating, smoking rooms and, sometimes, a dedicated fernery, providing enjoyment and instruction. When describing the new aquarium at Scarborough, the local paper wrote of how 'An aquarium is never a worn out novelty, but an ever-recurring source of amusement, intellectual study, and scientific gratification.'[11]

The seal-house at Edinburgh Aquarium was fitted up as a fernery, and *The Fishing Gazette* reported that 'the cavern-like places within it have a striking resemblance to a rocky shore, where successions of cavities and recesses of strange configuration and endless interest are to be met with. In this apartment four well-developed specimens of the seal may be seen disporting themselves in the water or resting on the rocky shelves forming the side of the tank.'[12] The contemporary Royal Aquarium in Rothesay on the Isle of Bute also had a seal house with 'luxuriant tree ferns'.[13] This is reminiscent of many private ferneries where wildlife, including birds, monkeys, goldfish, tortoises, lizards, toads, frogs and even alligators, was often to be found.

The two most impressive public coastal aquaria were designed by the prolific seaside architect Eugenius Birch. Brighton Aquarium was the first recreational aquarium in England. Work began in 1870, and the building was opened in 1872, having cost £133,000. It was sunk into the cliff face between Madeira Drive and Marine Parade, where the Palace Pier met the land. A sense of mystery and excitement was generated by having to descend twenty feet down a broad flight of granite steps from the ticket office into the gloomy subterranean interior.

As well as the marine exhibits (including seals and a Sumatran alligator), there was a reading room, naturalists' rooms and a restaurant. Facilities were expanded in 1876 to include a roller-skating rink on the roof terrace. At the eastern end was a conservatory, 160 feet long, 40 feet wide and 30 feet high, culminating in a fernery comprising a massive cliff of artificial rockwork with a cascade dropping over the top and forming pools at the base. It was 'chiefly intended as a lounge and resting-place and is plentifully decorated with every description of marine plants, polypiae, ferns, and miniature aquaria.'[14]

The rockwork was constructed by James Pulham & Son of Broxbourne in Hertfordshire. Their promotional booklet *Picturesque Ferneries and Rock-garden Scenery, in Waterfalls, Rocky-streams, Cascades, Dropping Wells, Heatheries, Caves or Cavernous Recesses for Boathouses &c., &c.,* published *c.*1877, lists nearly 200 works. The Pulhams made use of local stone whenever possible, but if it was not available they used a core of vitrified or burnt bricks (burrs or clinker) bound and rendered with a 'cement' that was known as Pulhamite. This was coloured to resemble indigenous rocks, and the artificial boulders were skilfully placed, modelled and carved to imitate the disposition and appearance of local natural stone.

The Art Journal thought that the fernery at Brighton was 'a model for all other undertakings of the kind, wherever executed . . . as evidence of what may be done in the way of grace and picturesque beauty in private grounds, small as well as large, and in extensive or moderately sized conservatories and ferneries,'[15] and concluded: 'Those [works executed by Pulham] that are in private grounds can be examined by few; those at Brighton will be seen by hundreds of thousands. . . .'[16] **(Fig. 7)**.

On 26 May 1877 the *Scarborough Mercury* chronicled 'an event probably unparalleled in the history of the town', the opening of the Scarborough Aquarium, which would 'afford another means of instruction and amusement to the masses.'[17] Birch's aquarium in this pre-eminent seaside resort lay beneath the Rotunda Museum and the Cliff Bridge. Under rows of skylights was a subterranean wonderland of arcades, courts and grottoes. Birch designed over

Fig. 7 The fernery at Brighton Aquarium from *The Art Journal*, December 1872. The lush vegetation, rocky outcrops, and nooks and corners of a fernery in a winter garden or aquarium provided a perfect location for a romantic rendezvous, as this sketch from *Judy* (1 November 1876) implies:

> 'Miss J: I consider the Brighton Aquarium a *great* institution. The Sea Lions are really awfully jolly, and the one who catches his dinner in his mouth standing up, and then barks and wags his dear old tail, is a perfect *duck*. Then, if one *does* happen to meet one's partner of the night before – quite by *accident*, of course – it *is* so convenient you know.
> Mr. S: Ya-as, oh, ya-as, *I* know. And do you know that cosy little corner in the fernery under the fountain – just chairs and woom enough for two, don't y'know?
> Miss J: (*ecstatically*). *Don't* I just! Oh *isn't* that a corner?
> Mr. S: (*with a sigh, and reflectively*). A – – – h! Isn't it just! . . . .

a dozen British piers, including Brighton's West Pier in 1866. This was the first in a vaguely oriental style that was subsequently deemed appropriate for seaside/relaxation buildings around the country. The architecture of Scarborough Aquarium was variously described as Mahomedan, Moorish,

Indian, Byzantine, and Arabesque. Like most 'Seaside Orientalism', it was eclectic and pure escapism. The *London Journal* thought that the building, when lighted up and crowded with visitors, had 'the appearance of a vast subterranean palace – the realization of one of the fairy creations of the "Arabian Nights Entertainments."'[18] As well as the expected fresh and sea-water tanks, ferns were an important element in the aquarium. *The Mercury* described how, once past the pay office and through the turnstile, the visitor followed a broad pathway lined with ornamental (possibly Pulhamite) rockwork, descended two flights of steps and passed a fernery and rockery with a dropping well, which was 'grand in its proportions and display'. But the main fernery was described as 'that miniature paradise'. It occupied the Central Court, which was 130 feet by 60 feet, lined with tufa, and with a cascade in one corner 'which comes splashing down from ledge to ledge amidst a perfect bower of ferns and tropical vegetation.' In another typical comment by the local press, the paper considered that 'we may almost consider that in Scarborough Aquarium we have reached the acme of perfection.' Sadly, the aquarium did not succeed and after decades of various uses, this fantastical Victorian seaside building was eventually demolished in the winter of 1968-9.

EXHIBITIONS

By the late nineteenth century it was almost a matter of course to have a rockwork fernery at an exhibition, either as one of the exhibits, or a place for relaxation and cooling refreshment. One of the prompts to the fern craze was the growth of the British Empire, which introduced gardeners to a huge range of exotic plants via travel and illustrations in books and periodicals. New and exciting flora and fauna were also displayed at shows, such as the Colonial and Indian Exhibition held in London in 1886, where there was a fernery in the New Zealand Court planted with native tree ferns (**Fig. 8**). This was created by Dick Radclyffe of High Holborn, a specialist in this type of work and manufacturer of fern cases, window cases, and aquaria.

Perhaps less predictably, ferneries (together with ice caverns, stalactite grottoes, and rockeries) were to be found at the Derby Fine Arts Exhibition of 1877 which, *The Art Journal* reported, 'added to the attractions and pleased many people.'[19] The International Health Exhibition held in 1884 in South Kensington also had 'good specimens of this comparatively new and charming art' of rockwork indoor ferneries.[20] Those in the Prince of Wales' Pavilions at the Paris Exhibition of 1878, the International Fisheries Exhibition of 1883, and the International Inventions Exhibition of 1885, the latter two also held at South Kensington, were also all executed by Dick Radclyffe & Co.

Unlike Pulham, Radclyffe was not concerned with geological accuracy, and produced picturesque rockwork ensembles that incorporated rustic stairways,

Fig. 8 The fernery in the New Zealand Court at the Colonial and Indian Exhibition, London, 1886, from *The Illustrated London News*.

arches, grottoes, and seats. *Myra's Journal of Dress and Fashion* thought the 'cool and delicious conservatory, with rockery, fernery, and a dripping well' at the Inventions Exhibition, completed the beauty of the 'miniature palace' that was the royal pavilion.[21]

POPULAR ENTERTAINMENT

This sort of fernery was particularly associated with music, dancing and drama. In the early 1870s the processional routes at Rivière's Covent Garden Promenade Concerts during the month of August, were lined with grottoes, ferneries (flanked with huge blocks of ice), and fountains, again constructed by Dick Radclyffe & Co. When A. & S. Gatti took over the concerts in 1874, they continued to provide these 'delightfully cool' alcoves and recesses in which to retire from the crush. These bucolic nooks emulated the ferneries created in the houses of the wealthy when they held dances. Such public and private ferneries were purely for pleasure: green, refreshing retreats from the heat of the crowd or ballroom. The educational aspect was totally absent and it was clearly not important what species of fern were planted on the rockwork.

When the Cremorne Pleasure Gardens in London re-opened for the 1860 season, one of the new features was a fernery with waterfalls and grottoes.

Even in a pleasure garden it was thought, perhaps naively, that besides being generally attractive this would 'afford a subject for interesting study.'[22] However, it did have to compete for attention against 'a dwarf, named Mahomed Bux, a native of Calcutta, who was present at the Cawnpore massacre, and whose life was only saved by his diminutiveness. . . .'[23]

Winter gardens, and even aquaria, were often used for concerts, with varying degrees of success. *Punch* commented, in its usual style, on the Winter Garden at Bournemouth in 1897: 'It is conceivable that there may be a better place for sound than this same Hothouse, where the orchestral performers appear as it were planted amidst the ferns, and may be individually and collectively considered as an essential portion of the Fern-iture.'[24] In 1869 alterations were carried out at the Prince of Wales' Theatre in London, including the remarkable act of moving the orchestra to sit beneath the stage:

> an opening by the footlights allowing the sound of the music to be as distinctly heard as heretofore. ... The space formerly occupied by the band is now converted into a grotto and fernery, intended, with fountains and jets of water, to cool the atmosphere between the acts, and by an ingenious looking-glass arrangement to exhibit an interminably multiplied reflection of tiny crystal rills, which will leap and sparkle in the light through a multitude of leafy labyrinths constructed out of tangled masses of choice ferns most artistically disposed.

The writer concluded: 'The device is excessively pretty and tasteful; and we look to see it generally imitated.'[25] The views of the members of the orchestra are not recorded. A similar plan seems to have been proposed at the Kibble Palace glasshouse after it was transported from John Kibble's home on the Clyde estuary to Glasgow Botanic Gardens in 1872. Once re-erected and enlarged by James Boyd & Sons, it housed an important collection of tree ferns. Reporting on the grand opening, *The Glasgow Herald* stated that:

> Underneath the pond is a chamber 14 feet in diameter, where it is proposed to place an orchestra, whose music will form a melodious mystery . . . The chamber will be so constructed that the sounds of the instruments may be admitted or shut out of the dome at will, and in this way it is expected that charming diminuendo and crescendo effects will be obtained from the invisible performers. When this artifice is not employed, it is intended to place in the centre of the pond a fairy fountain which will throw up 40 jets of water to a height of 35 feet while electric lights placed on the roof will be directed upon the rising and falling spray, tinting it with changing hues of gold and silver and all the colours of the rainbow.[26]

Perhaps the Scottish musicians refused to cooperate, as there are no reports of this sub-marine arrangement being carried out, although the chamber existed, and was used for 'manipulating the prismatic effects of the Grand Fairy Fountain'.[27]

In the 1870s and '80s both the Pavilion and Lyceum Theatres in London were remodelled, and ferneries – presumably rockwork ensembles with fountains etc. – together with other rich decorations, introduced. At the newly-built Prince's Theatre in London in 1884, a grotto and fernery actually extended under the pavement of the street outside (**Fig. 9**). *The Theatre* wondered whether these 'Lounges, corridors, fountains, ferns, drawing-rooms, retiring-rooms, smoking-rooms, annexes, marble halls and staircases, Moorish decorations and so on', would prove more attractive than the play itself. But they realised that 'The Theatre becomes the most popular that is the smartest, and the outside show is considered more important than the actual entertainment.'[28] *Judy* commented that Henry Irving, the manager of the Lyceum, 'fully appreciates the importance of "working the parade." In the race for taste he has certainly distanced all the theatro-artistic contingent of London with his Arabian palace for an entrance.'[29]

FERNERIES EVERYWHERE?

The extent of the fern craze in mainstream Victorian and Edwardian society can be seen from the huge variety of places where it was considered appropriate to erect a fernery. Not surprisingly, they featured in public gardens, from the ornamental promenade grounds laid out at the new resort of St Anne's-on-the-Sea in 1875, to the little oasis created in the 1880s by the Rev.

Fig. 9 The Prince's Theatre in London was designed by C.J. Phipps, and opened in 1884. *The British Architect* of 18 January 1884 described how 'situated under the pavement of the street is a grotto and fernery specially for gentlemen.' This segregation of the sexes appears to have been dispensed with at the time of this engraving.

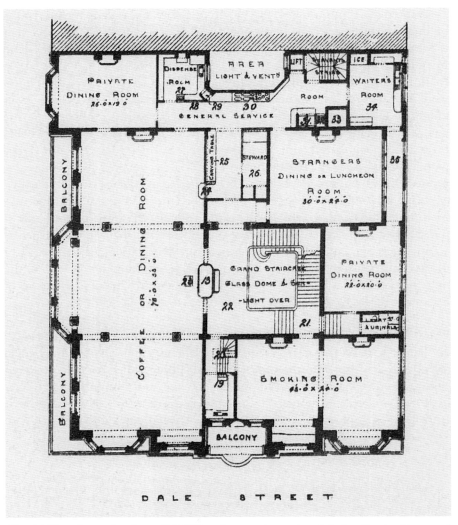

Fig. 10 First-floor plan from C.O. Ellison's second premiated design for the Liverpool Conservative Club. The fernery is marked as no. 13 in the centre of the plan (*British Architect*, 29 October 1880).

Sidney Vatcher next to the church of St Philip, Stepney, in the East End, for the poor members of his parish.

Perhaps more unexpectedly, at the Liverpool Young Men's Christian Association building, opened in 1877, the south end of the reading room led into a fernery. No doubt it was thought that this would aid both the young men's spiritual and intellectual improvement. The second-prize entry for a new Conservative Club in the city in 1880 was designed by C.O. Ellison as a huge Italianate palazzo. It featured 'large elegant ferneries' placed in the middle of the double doors between the morning room and entrance hall on the ground floor, and the dining room and grand staircase on the first. *The British Architect* believed that the beauty of the effect of looking through the enormous glass cases full of foliage 'into the noble rooms, or from the rooms to the grand staircase and dome', was 'too apparent to need further pointing out.'[30] (**Fig. 10**). Even so, in the Fulham Baths Competition of 1899, the assessor 'was not to be beguiled from his wise thoughts by the seductions of a perambulator-shed and a fernery!' provided in one entry.[31]

Perhaps most appropriately for a person suffering from Pteridomania, or fern madness, Wardian cases were installed in some of the huge number of Victorian lunatic asylums. Nathaniel Ward believed that window cases might be made 'the means of illustrating the antiquities of any country – by erecting in them models of old towers, castles, gateways, &c., and which, when covered with plants, would form *tableaux vivans* of the highest interest.'[32] He particularly thought that such cases set into the walls of the depressing long corridors

Fig. 11 The Gallery for Women at Bethlem Hospital with Wardian cases filling the lower quarters of the inside of alternate windows along the corridor. (*Illustrated London News*, 24 March 1860).

Fig. 12 The Gallery for Men at Bethlem Hospital. It too has Wardian cases which fill the lower quarters of the inside of windows along the corridor, and which alternate with aviaries. (*Illustrated London News*, 24 March 1860).

of asylums would change them into 'one of the most beautiful promenades conceivable,' and thereby soothe the afflicted.[33]

By the second half of the nineteenth century, providing a 'homely' environment in lunatic asylums had become the norm, and interiors even reflected changing fashions in domestic design. It was also believed that a high-quality environment with a plethora of objects of interest would have a humanising effect on patients that would help keep them calm. From the 1850s significant programmes of reform were instigated at Bethlem Hospital in Southwark (**Figs. 11, 12**), with increasing provision for occupation and entertainment. In 1860 *The Lady's Newspaper* reported that:

> Everything that can enliven and distract has been imagined with ingenious forethought, and placed there to chase away gloom and melancholy, the too natural attributes of such an abode; gold-fish in glass globes, embedded in bright green moss, vivaria, fountains, aviaries, pet animals in cages, ferneries are fixed in the embrasures of the windows, serving the double purpose of rendering their approach difficult, and adding to the interest of the occupant.'[34]

Notes

1. The Rev. Charles Kingsley (1819-75) first used the term Pteridomania in his book, *Glaucus; Or, the Wonders of the Shore,* Cambridge, 1855, pp. 4-5. It comes from the term pteridophytes, the group of vascular plants that reproduce by spores, i.e. ferns, and what were then classified as the fern allies: clubmosses, spikemosses, pepperworts, quillworts, whisk ferns, and horsetails.

2. Edward Newman, *A History of British Ferns,* London, 1840, pp. x-xi.

3. 'A New Fernery', *The Garden*, 20 February 1875, p. 151.

4. Quoted in Eileen McCracken, *The Palm House and Botanic Garden, Belfast,* Belfast, 1971, p. 44.

5. 'Architectural, Engineering, and Local Public Works', *The British Architect*, 21 May 1875, p. 292.

6. 'Architectural, Engineering, and Local Public Works', *The British Architect*, 14 April 1876, pp. 191-5 (p. 194).

7. *Southport: Descriptive & Illustrative,* 3rd edition, London, 1901, p. 28.

8. *The Era Almanack Advertiser*, January 1889, p. 116.

9. Ibid., January 1892, p. 116.

10. Shirley Hibberd, *Rustic Adornments for Homes of Taste: And Recreations for Town Folk in the Study and Imitation of Nature,* London, 1856, p. 121.

11. 'Opening of The Scarborough Aquarium: Full Description of the Building', *Scarborough Mercury,* 26 May 1877, p. 4.

12. 'Angler-Naturalist', *The Fishing Gazette: An Illustrated Journal for Anglers, Fishermen & Angler-Naturalist*, 16 August 1878, p. 390.

13. *See* Anne Neale, 'The Garden Designs of Edward La Trobe Bateman (1816-97)', *Garden History*, 33:2, Winter 2005, pp. 225-55 (p. 247).

14. The Brighton Aquarium on the Formal Opening Day', *Illustrated London News*, 10 August 1872, p. 123.

15. S.C. Hall, 'The Aquarium at Brighton', *The Art Journal*, December 1872, pp. 310-12 (p. 311).

16. *The Art Journal*, December 1872, p. 312.

17. *Scarborough Mercury,* 26 May 1877, p. 4.

18. 'Scarborough and its Aquarium', *London Journal*, 15 September 1877, p. 165.

19. 'The Derby Fine Arts Exhibition', *The Art Journal*, November 1877, p. 341.

20. James Sheppard, 'Rock, Alpine, Fern, and Wild Gardening: The In-door Fernery', pp. 218-23, in D. T. Fish, *Cassell's Popular Gardening*, vol. III, London, New York & Melbourne, n.d. [1884-6], p. 218.

21. 'The Inventions Exhibition', *Myra's Journal of Dress & Fashion*, 1 July 1885, p. 350.

22. *Bell's Life in London and Sporting Chronicle*, 20 May 1860, p. 8.

23. *John Bull and Britannia*, 12 May 1860, p. 301.

24. 'Down South', *Punch*, 28 August 1897, p. 94.

25. 'The Theatres', *The Orchestra*, 17 September 1869, p. 404-5 (p. 404).

26. *Glasgow Herald*, 7 May 1873, quoted in Eric W. Curtis, *Kibble's Palace,* Glendaruel, 1999, p. 31.

27. Curtis (note 26), p. 32.

28. 'The Palace of Truth', *The Theatre*, 1 February 1884, pp. 88-91 (p. 89).

29. 'The Only Jones', *Judy*, 1 February 1882, p. 52.

30. 'Second Premiated Design for the Liverpool Conservative Club', *The British Architect*, 29 October 1880, p. 196.

31. 'Fulham Baths Competition', *The British Architect*, 17 November 1899, pp. 341–2 (p. 342).

32. N.B. Ward, *On the Growth of Plants in Closely Glazed Cases,* 2nd edition, London, 1852, p. 94.

33. Ibid., pp. 114–15.

34. 'Bethlehem Hospital', *The Lady's Newspaper*, 7 April 1860, p. 277.

3 Patriotic Pleasures: Boathouses and Boating in the English Lakes

ADAM MENUGE

In 1843 the poet William Wordsworth dictated to his loyal amanuensis Isabella Fenwick the circumstances surrounding the composition of many of his poems. In the course of describing the characters and incidents of his long poem *The Excursion* (1814) he gave vent to a complaint about one Dr William Pearson (1767–1847), once his schoolfellow at Hawkshead Grammar School but now the owner of a small villa estate overlooking the small lake of Grasmere. Pearson, he complained,

> is now erecting a boat-house with an upper story to be resorted to as an entertaining-room when he & his associates may feel inclined to take their pastime on the Lake. Every Passenger will be disgusted with the sight of this Edifice not merely as a tasteless thing in itself, but as utterly out of place & peculiarly fitted as far as it is observed (& it obtrudes itself on notice at every point of view) to mar the beauty & destroy the pastoral simplicity of the Vale. ... I will only add that as the foundation has twice failed from the Lake no doubt being intolerant of the intrusion there is some ground for hoping that the impertinent structure will not stand.[1]

Wordsworth lived nearby at Rydal Mount, a residence overlooking Rydal Water and a stretch of Windermere rather than Grasmere. But previously, between 1799 and 1813, he had lived at three different houses in the Vale of Grasmere, at the first of which – Dove Cottage – he had been in the habit of composing on the lake shore close to where the offending boathouse was now erecting.

Pearson's boathouse has endured, thwarting Wordsworth's hopes of a swift demise (**Fig. 1**). It was an accompaniment to his recently built villa, How Top, which commanded enviable views of the lake from the slope rising above the boathouse. Pearson's was not the first boathouse in the secluded Vale of Grasmere, which since the poet Thomas Gray sang its praises in 1769 had been invested by writers and artists with an overwhelming burden of pastoral

Fig. 1 William Pearson's 1843 boathouse, serving How Top, Grasmere. [Author].

associations. The 1843 Grasmere tithe map, which shows How Top and its boathouse, also shows another boathouse on the opposite side of the lake.[2] This served a former farmhouse which had been extended in 1809 to serve as a small villa known as Dale End. The nearby boathouse (**Fig. 2**), utterly vernacular in its random rubble masonry and Cumbrian slate roof, is very likely of the same date. The curious apsidal landward end, which marks it out as a villa-owner's toy, may be a later addition.

Why should Grasmere's second boathouse provoke such opprobrium? Wordsworth's outrage must have been triggered by some more particular smart than the sense that a favourite lakeside haunt had been violated. In fact the tranquillity of the lake shore had been laid open and despoiled as long ago as the 1820s with the building of a new length of turnpike road through the vale. What seems most to have roused Wordsworth's ire was the news that Pearson's boathouse would be used 'as an entertaining-room' for 'associates'. The upper floor is well-lit, with one window occupying the gable facing the lake and another in a south-facing dormer, and it is heated on the north wall by a fireplace served by a tall, circular chimney (loosely based on the form commended by Wordsworth as rooted in the local vernacular tradition).[3] While the Dale End boathouse had been a simple single-storey stone shed, Pearson's introduced a new mode of enjoying the once quiet lake shore and, perhaps, of prolonging entertainment noisily into the night. In the contrast between the two boathouses lies the story of how the Victorian boathouse parted company from its late eighteenth- and early nineteenth-century forebears.

THE FIRST LAKE DISTRICT BOATHOUSES

While it might seem sensible to equate the presence of boats with the need for boathouses to shelter and secure them, the truth is somewhat different. The English Lakes were worked for centuries if not millennia by small oared or sailing craft designed for fishing, carrying cargo such as slate, timber or bark, and ferrying passengers – as on the Windermere Ferry, documented since the seventeenth century. Few if any of these craft were afforded the luxury of a boathouse. As a general rule working boats, plainly and robustly built, were left open to the elements in all weathers, either moored in the water or drawn up on the shore. The need for boathouses only arose when boats fitted out especially for pleasure began to ply the waters, because pleasure craft could be highly decorated and equipped with more or less costly furnishings – features which would be impaired by prolonged exposure to the weather.

The origins of the boathouse are rooted in a long-established tradition of exploiting the Lakeland landscape as a game preserve. The Hasell family of Dalemain, for example, kept a boathouse on Ullswater. Their boat was used to ferry hunting parties en route between the house, situated a little below the foot of the lake, and the bleak hunting ground of Martindale, where they maintained a primitive lodge (described in 1805 as 'fitted up in the Sportsman's style')[4] in which simple refreshments could be taken. On a somewhat grander scale Charles Howard, earl of Surrey and later 11th duke of Norfolk, kept a

Fig. 2 The boathouse at Dale End, Grasmere, probably *c.*1809, is typical of many early Lake District boathouses with its elongated plan, low eaves and absence of windows; the apsidal landward end is unusual. [Author].

boat to service Lyulph's Tower, his Gothic hunting lodge beside Ullswater. An early description of the boat makes clear that it was used for one of the characteristic pastimes of early Lakes tourists – discharging guns in order to enjoy the echoes reverberating from the surrounding mountains: the boat, 'which the Earl of Surrey politely gives leave to his keeper to accommodate any gentleman who desires it[,] … is adapted for eight rowers, (for whom there are likewise caps and shirts,) and mounts twelve brass swivel guns, for the purpose of trying the echoes: the pay of the rowers here is 2s. a day for each man, and they are always provided with ammunition for the guns'.[5]

In making his boat available to others the earl of Surrey may have been emulating the dukes of Portland, who held the Honour of Penrith, including the former royal preserve of Inglewood Forest, and who had a boathouse on Ullswater by the early 1770s. This survives, albeit converted to provide holiday accommodation on the upper floor (**Fig. 3**). The antiquarian William Hutchinson, who toured the Lakes in 1773, noted that on the Ullswater leg of his excursion

> We were accommodated on the water with one of the barges belonging to the Duke of Portland, which have been sent there by his grace for pleasuring … Whilst we sat to regale [i.e. take lunch], the barge put off from shore, to a station where the finest echoes were to be obtained from the surrounding mountains. – The vessel was provided with six brass cannon, mounted on swivels; – on the discharge of one of these pieces, the report was echoed from the opposite rocks, where by reverberation it seemed to roll from cliff to cliff, and return through every cave and valley; till the decreasing tumult gradually died away upon the ear.

Fig. 3 The duke of Portland's boathouse near Pooley Bridge, Ullswater. [Author].

Later the party enjoyed a variation on the entertainment, in which the music of French horns replaced the sound of gunfire.[6]

THE IMPACT OF VILLA BUILDING

The vast majority of Lake District boathouses were built, not to serve the recreational needs of nearby aristocratic and gentry estates, but to service the villas which proliferated from the 1770s onwards, most of them built to house wealthy incomers who had acquired the fashionable appetite for mountain and lake scenery. While these villas varied enormously in scale, from the magnificent to the modest, most strove to establish a visual connection with one of the lakes. Nearly all the larger and more prestigious examples, as well as many smaller villas, enjoyed a lake frontage and had at least one boathouse.

Two houses stand out in the early history of Lake District villas, each achieving a certain notoriety among contemporaries. Belle Isle was built on Windermere's largest island from 1774 by Thomas English, described in deeds as a 'founder' of St Pancras.[7] He employed a London architect, John Plaw, to design one of the most remarkable villas of its age, circular on plan beneath a domed roof, with a series of windows offering entrancingly varied views of the lake and its environs, and a temple front facing the approach across the water from Bowness. The accompanying boathouse is a vernacular affair by comparison – a long stone shed with a large timber-lintelled water entrance in one gable wall and in the other a small land entrance beneath a blind Venetian window. The three-bay roof retains its original stout oak trusses but the interior is otherwise entirely plain (**Fig. 4**).

Belle Isle attracted hostile comment from contemporaries who resented its intrusion into an already treasured landscape. But the precedent was not lost on Joseph Pocklington, wealthy son of a Newark banker, who in 1778 built a house to his own designs on the largest island on Derwent Water.

Fig. 5 Derwent Isle, formerly Pocklington's Island, Keswick: the landing stage, porter's lodge and house, from an engraving, dated 1786, based on an original 'Drawn upon the Spot by Joseph Pocklington'. [Author's collection].

Pocklington was both a showman, promoting some of the earliest regattas on Derwent Water, and a zealous self-publicist who documented his works in a series of engravings published in William Hutchinson's *History of Cumberland*.[8] Besides his relatively modest bachelor villa, now known as Derwent Isle, Pocklington created a fantastic island landscape peppered with ornamental and sham structures, including a fort, 'Saint Mary's Church', a boathouse, a lodge, a 'Druid's Stone' and a 'Druid Temple' or stone circle 56 feet in diameter. Contemporaries, no better disposed towards Pocklington than they had been towards English, heaped derision on his efforts, most of which were swept away soon after he sold the estate *circa* 1797, if not before.

Pocklington's boathouse does not survive, but its form is recorded on a map published by him in 1783.[9] This indicates the position of the boathouse, and includes a view of what must be the landward elevation. It is a simple Gothic composition with pointed-arched openings disposed symmetrically in a gable wall rising steeply to a bell-cote surmounted by a cross. Like its precursor at Belle Isle the Derwent Isle boathouse was positioned well away from the formal approach to the house, which was via a landing stage next to the porter's lodge (**Fig. 5**), and was only a little closer to another landing stage next to St Mary's church, one of Pocklington's more exuberant pieces of whimsy. Visitors disembarked in front of the house, in much the same way as if descending from their carriages at the front steps. A boat could be moored in readiness at one of the landing stages, but for more prolonged periods it would be removed and berthed in the boathouse, as horses and carriages would be removed to the stable yard until needed. Whatever refinements such boats might display, their care, maintenance and crewing were servile occupations which should not obtrude upon the polite gaze. Pocklington's boathouse presented a fashionable elevation to those viewing his creations from the mainland just 200 metres away, but in essence the boathouse of this era had few pretensions.

THE NAUTICAL CULTURE OF THE ENGLISH LAKES

After Derwent Isle no more island villas were built, so it was quite abnormal for villa owners to depend utterly on the presence of boats. But for many, travel by water represented, if not a necessity, then a very considerable convenience when compared with land transport. As late as the 1840s many visits to the Lake District began with, or incorporated, a coastwise journey, often from Liverpool to Milnthorpe or another haven on Morecambe Bay. The ribbon-like form of lakes such as Windermere, Coniston Water and Ullswater made for very long and roundabout journeys by road; the same journeys could often be accomplished in a fraction of the time by water. A number of villa owners came to rely heavily on water communication. Most famously, from 1870 Henry W. Schneider (1817-87), the Swiss-descended iron-founder, commuted from Belsfield, his Bowness villa, by taking his Glasgow-built steam yacht *Esperance* half the length of Windermere before continuing his journey by train from Lakeside, near Newby Bridge, to his iron works in Barrow-in-Furness.[10]

For the majority of villa-dwellers, however, the lakes were a playground first and foremost. Early writers, extolling the scenic virtues of the area, laid great stress on the importance of obtaining contrasting views of the landscape – from the summit of Skiddaw, from notable vantage points, more commonly at a modest elevation above the lake, and from the surface of the lake itself. For many, sightseeing was a peaceful and contemplative pursuit but it could also be enlivened, as we have seen, by the discharge of gunshot and other amusements. Most tours involved a boat trip on at least one of the major lakes – Windermere, Derwent Water or Ullswater. As Lake District tourism became increasingly commercialised it became normal to hire a boat and boatman

Fig. 6 Storrs Hall, Windermere, and the Temple of the Heroes, engraved by W. Tombleson and first published in 1831 by John and Frederick Harwood. The boat to the left of the Temple would be described in the early nineteenth century as a barge. [Author's collection].

from one of the hotels or inns. The boats used varied widely in size from small rowing boats to substantial oared barges and swifter yachts.

In 1782 the Keswick cartographer and museum proprietor, Peter Crosthwaite (1735-1808), began publishing his series of lake maps for tourists.[11] Crosthwaite sponsored regattas on Derwent Water, and similar events were staged on Windermere, where boat races remained popular throughout the nineteenth century. The early regattas were boisterous affairs involving mock-battles as well as races, the former rendered more credible by stage scenery such as Pocklington's 'fort', by the use of small cannon and pyrotechnics, and by the enlistment of large numbers of servants and 'extras'. While such antics are easily ridiculed they expressed something of the nervousness attending international affairs in the Age of Revolution. The English Lakes were an arena in which all sorts of feelings, ranging from merely puerile high jinks to the profounder depths of patriotism, could be played out. The lakes were figured as miniature inland seas, and a play of defending their shores enacted the wider struggle against periodically threatening European powers.

It was in this climate, while the Royal Navy formed the nation's principal line of defence, that Sir John Legard, an East Riding landowner, built his 'Temple of the Heroes'. Standing at the end of a stone pier extending from the promontory on which Storrs Hall, his villa, had been built in the mid-1790s, this small but prominently positioned building commemorates Admirals Duncan, Nelson, Howe and St Vincent (**Fig. 6**).[12] The undated Temple was in existence by about 1802 and the date of construction can be narrowed down by reference to the naval careers that it invokes. Admiral Duncan (1731–1804) was the victor of Camperdown, an engagement with the Dutch fleet in 1797; Admiral Howe (1726–99) came to prominence in 1794 for an inconclusive but nonetheless celebrated action against the French fleet known as the Glorious First of June; John Jervis, 1st earl of St Vincent, took his title from the Battle of Cape St Vincent in 1797, when he defeated the Spanish fleet off the coast of Portugal; Nelson's career, needless to say, had not fully run its course, but he had already come to prominence at the Battle of Cape St Vincent, in recognition of which he was promoted to the rank of Rear Admiral, and he achieved fame the following year with his defeat of the French at the Battle of the Nile on 1 August 1798. Thus the careers of the four admirals, taken together, point to a likely construction date for the Temple in the year or two following the Battle of the Nile.

It is therefore a matter of conjecture whether the Temple of the Heroes preceded or post-dated Finsthwaite Tower, an eye-catcher and belvedere crowning a hilltop overlooking the southern end of Windermere, which is dated by inscription to 1799.[13] Finsthwaite Tower was erected by James King of Finsthwaite House with a strikingly similar intention: 'To Honor the Officers, Seamen and Marines of the ROYAL NAVY, whose matchless Conduct, and irresistible Valour, decisively defeated the Fleets of France, Spain, and Holland, and preserved and protected LIBERTY *and* COMMERCE'. Claife Station, originally also a freestanding tower, but octagonal rather than square, was built to John Carr's designs in the same year,[14] and although avowedly a belvedere rather than a monument to naval prowess it commands the lake shore like another fortlet, and indeed received castellated additions shortly after it was first built. Together the three towers conjured a spirit of national resistance, and it was against this backdrop that Windermere entered the nineteenth century. Something of the same embattled determination lingered on through the later alarms occasioned by the agitation for constitutional reform, by the Continental revolutions of 1830 and 1848, and by later invasion scares, so that the castellated boathouses which increasingly lined the shores of Windermere and other lakes similarly assumed a mantle of national defence (**Fig. 7**). Messing about in boats had become a patriotic duty.

Patriotic fervour came to a head on two notable occasions. One was the celebrated regatta hosted in 1825 by John Bolton (who had acquired, and greatly extended, Storrs Hall) and organised by John Wilson (the 'Christopher North' of *Blackwood's Magazine* and a noted yachtsman) in honour of Sir Walter Scott's birthday, when the illustrious company also included William

Fig. 7 The defended shore: Monk Coniston Hall, Coniston, a castellated summer house to its right, and the Gothic boathouse in the right foreground, as depicted in a lithograph (Binns & Co., after a sketch by J. G. Binns) included with the 1835 sale particulars. [Cumbria Record Office (Kendal), WDX/745].

Wordsworth, George Canning (then Foreign Secretary) and James Lockhart (later Scott's biographer). The other was the visit of Queen Adelaide, the Queen Dowager, who visited the Lake District in 1840.

Queen Adelaide (1792-1849) was the eldest daughter of George, duke of Saxe-Coburg Meiningen, and the widow of William IV. Details of her visit to the Lakes are contained in a contemporary newspaper account.[15] The queen reached Kirkby Lonsdale on Thursday 23 July with an entourage including her sister, the duchess of Saxe-Weimar. On the following day they travelled by Milnthorpe and Newby Bridge to Bowness, where the queen was accommodated at Ullock's White Lion Hotel and was 'respectfully received by a number of the first gentlemen in the neighbourhood'. On Saturday 25 July the queen visited Storrs Hall, where she was the guest of Colonel Bolton's widow, who also provided the barge in which the party were then conveyed.

They were rowed to the Lowwood Inn, where there was a further 'right loyal reception by all the gentry', followed by a dinner, after which the party returned to Bowness. Sunday was taken up by church attendances, followed by a trip, once again in Mrs Bolton's barge, to the home of the Flemings at Rayrigg Hall. Here the Queen was conducted to a noted viewpoint or 'station' on Rayrigg Bank, subsequently renamed Queen Adelaide's Hill, before departing for a boat trip around Belle Isle and a visit to Claife Station, returning to Bowness again in the evening. On Monday 27 July the party went to Rydal, where the Queen met the Wordsworths at the waterfalls in Rydal Park, and witnessed a rush-bearing ceremony at the church before proceeding first to Keswick for a boat trip on Derwent Water, and thence to Patterdale where the party was conducted around the Aira Force gardens. On the final day of a punishing schedule dominated by nautical excursions the royal party was conveyed via Bowness to Levens Hall, and onward to Lancaster.

The boats which appear in countless early-nineteenth-century engravings embrace a range of types. On the smaller lakes where winds were quixotic rowing boats predominated, though some might have provision for hoisting a small mast. Many small boathouses, such as that serving The Lea, Grasmere, were built to house these diminutive craft (**Fig. 8**). On the larger lakes such boats were supplemented by two further types of pleasure boat. Oared barges were favoured for sight-seeing parties and entertaining, offering stability in the water and the freedom to erect an awning or canopy to protect passengers from sun or light rain. Sailing yachts were designed with racing and other muscular exertions in mind. Schooner-rigged yachts with two masts were popular in the second quarter of the nineteenth century but by the middle of the century something approaching the modern single-masted yacht, with a capacious foresail, was becoming common. Many early yachts were built

Fig. 8 Built for The Lea, Grasmere, this boathouse is typical of mid-nineteenth-century provision for small craft on the lesser lakes. A short channel links the boathouse with the lake. [Author].

away from the Lake District in established maritime boat-building centres, and fishermen from Morecambe were hired as crews. From the middle of the 19th century steam propulsion became widespread: a commercial wooden-hulled paddle-steamer, *Lady of the Lake*, was launched on Windermere in 1845, to be joined a year later by the iron-hulled *Lord of the Isles*.[16] Steam yachts were not far behind. They were primarily not for racing, but for cruising and entertaining, and most were too large to take advantage of boathouses. The earlier oared barges gave way to steam launches. Larger examples, like the sleek *SS Gondola* on Coniston Water, might be fitted with permanent cabins, but small launches remained vulnerable to the weather and continued to be kept in boathouses.

THE BOATHOUSE: CHARACTERISTIC FEATURES

The purpose of the boathouse is simple: to shelter boats from the destructive effects of wind, rain, frost and sunlight, and to secure them from accidental or malicious damage. At the same time the boathouse provides a certain amount of space for storing associated equipment such as oars, masts and sails, and it enables certain works of maintenance, repair or minor alteration to be carried out under cover. Boathouses are not used for boat-building or for substantial repairs, for which a boat yard or slip, whether covered or not, is required.

The vast majority of Lake District boathouses have no further ambitions than these. Their essential requirements are equally simple: one or more water entrances, wide enough for the type of craft intended, and often buttressed to either side; a land entrance; an internal stage, either fixed or floating, along one end or, preferably, one or more sides of the boathouse; and sufficient space either along the walls, in a loft, or suspended from the roof, to store

Fig. 9 The wet boathouse at Wansfell Holme, Ambleside, dated 1866, has a wide roof descending to low eaves, creating enough space for stone stages (one of them largely collapsed) along both sides, with ample light from windows in the gable wall facing the lake. This boathouse was badly damaged by floods in November 2009. [Author].

any equipment or materials not conveniently carried on the boat itself. The main sources of light were often the two entrances, when open, sometimes supplemented by slit vents or a gable window. Light from the water entrance was often increased by fitting slatted (rather than solid) wooden doors. From the mid–nineteenth century onwards it became common to build boathouses with stages of more generous width, lit by windows usually in the lakeside gable wall. The boathouse at Wansfell Holme, Ambleside, dated 1866, takes this form which, coupled with the steeply pitched Gothic roofs of the period, brings the eaves almost down to ground level (**Fig. 9**).

The siting of boathouses was carefully considered. Where possible they take advantage of natural bays or inlets which provide some protection against storms and (particularly since the advent of steam propulsion in the 1840s) wash from passing craft. Many are associated with modest engineering works such as a revetment encroaching on the lake (to gain depth for moorings), or a short channel designed to eliminate lakeside shallows (one of the longest, better deserving the name 'canal', is at Storrs Hall). The Wray Castle boathouse is protected by a substantial artificial promontory doubling as a quay and incorporating an open wet dock. In nearly all cases, boathouses are set to one side of the main visual axis to and from the house with which they are associated so as not to clutter the view. They are a picturesque feature of the lake shore, and their lake elevations are invariably the most ornate, but their rear ends are usually *sans culottes*.

A NEW PROMINENCE: WRAY CASTLE

The boathouse acquired a new presence in the early decades of the nineteenth century. Liberated from the strictures of classical architecture it began to express the native slate and carboniferous limestone of the lake shores and to acquire, in many cases, a modest veil of Gothic styling. As the century progressed, a more central role for sport and physical recreation in the lives of the better off helped to redefine the boathouse as something on the same social axis as the villa presiding over it.

The history of Wray Castle offers an early expression of this altered social geography. Built from 1840 by James Dawson, an eminent Liverpool surgeon, using money inherited by his wife Margaret (*née* Preston) from her family's distilling business, Wray Castle stands on the quieter western shore of Windermere, and is the crude but undoubtedly powerful creation of an almost unknown Liverpool architect, John Jackson Lightfoot.[17]

Details of the Dawsons' social life at Wray Castle are sketchy, but it is clear that they made the estate a centre for the wider family, especially on the Preston side through which the property eventually descended. Although Dawson was in his sixties when he moved there, and is not known to have had any nautical interests, one of his Preston relations acquired a 20-ton yacht, *Hebe*, which had enjoyed a successful racing career on the Solent since she was built at Cowes around 1839. Such a boat, which would be unsuitable for more sedate recreations, may account for the size of the boathouse at Wray Castle, which was built shortly after 1847 (and several years after Lightfoot's death), and had berths for two or three substantial craft. In 1850 Francis Dukinfield Palmer Astley, the owner of Fell Foot, a villa near the southern tip of Windermere, offered a prize for a yachting race. Like many prize-givers, Astley stipulated that the finishing line should be in full view of his property, where he doubtless assembled a large company for the occasion (the Revd Thomas Staniforth, who lived at Storrs Hall from 1859 to 1887, once decreed that an entire race should be visible from the Temple of the Heroes). *Hebe* won the race by a substantial margin but lost on handicap. While clearly a formidable competitor, she was judged ill-suited to local conditions. Described as 'the largest sailing craft ever seen upon the lake', it was said that 'her draft of water was so great that she could not pass through the Narrows except with a fair wind and when the lake was high[;] she was found to be too large and unwieldy for the lake, and for years she was laid up in the Wray boathouse'. Eventually another yachtsman, William Forwood, acquired her as a 'cruiser' or pleasure yacht.[18]

Wray Castle is unusual among Windermere villas in wearing the full panoply of the landed estate. In addition to what is probably the largest private boathouse on Windermere, extensive landscaped grounds, mock-ruins, garden buildings and the inevitable stable and coach house it boasts a secondary residence, an estate church and vicarage, and an imposing Gothic gate lodge. The lodge opened on to a long sinuous drive which, in characteristic picturesque fashion, defers the *coup-de-théatre* of extensive views over Windermere until the last minute. It is an impressive approach, but it enters the estate on the west side and many visitors, especially once the Kendal & Windermere Railway opened its Birthwaite (now Windermere) terminus in 1847, must have approached across the lake from the eastern shore. Unlike the late-eighteenth-century boathouses we have discussed, the Wray Castle boathouse is fully integrated into the experience offered to visitors to the house, which it echoes stylistically (**Fig. 10**). From the boathouse a path follows a gentle winding ascent, passing beneath the bristling mock-ruins or out-works of the towering house, and eventually climbing a series of stairs to emerge in front of the *porte-cochère*. No longer the humble and secluded berth for the owner's boats, the Wray Castle boathouse punctuates the approach by water in the same way that the gate lodge does the approach by land.

At Hallsteads, the Ullswater villa built for the Leeds industrialist and friend of the Wordsworths, John Marshall, the boathouse as lodge assumes a more explicit form. Here the gate lodge and one of the estate boathouses are combined in a single building arranged on a T-plan, the boathouse and well-lit room over forming the stem of the 'T' while the living accommodation, on two storeys, forms the remainder, flanking the approach to the house from Patterdale. With its exposed slate rubble and quoins the building, present by 1861, is unlikely to date from before 1840, and is perhaps the work not of John Marshall but of his youngest son Arthur, who inherited Hallsteads in 1845. The triplet of rounded chimneys can probably be attributed to Wordsworth's fondness for this feature of the local vernacular.[19]

THE SPORTING LIFE: FELL FOOT

A further enlargement of ambition can be seen in the complex history of the boathouses at Fell Foot, near the southern tip of Windermere.[20] From 1619 until 1785 Fell Foot belonged to the Robinson family, who built what was described in the latter year, when the property was put up for sale, as a 'large and convenient Mansion-house' amid gardens, orchards, a farmhouse and about 80 acres of arable and woodland. The advertisement, placed as far afield as London, was carefully worded to attract lovers of Lake District scenery, pointing out that 'The Situation of this Estate, and its natural Beauties, have always been greatly and justly admired, and it is still capable of many ornamental improvements in the Hands of a Person of Taste'.[21] The purchaser was Jeremiah Dixon, a Leeds merchant who is generally thought to have been the builder of a large villa which was demolished in or shortly after 1907. With its long lake frontage Fell Foot must have acquired a boathouse when the villa was first built or soon afterwards. The earliest of the existing boathouses corresponds to a building shown on the Cartmel enclosure map surveyed in 1807 and probably dates from before 1800.[22]

The Fell Foot estate was sold before 1813 to Francis Dukinfield Astley, a

Fig. 10 The huge boathouse at Wray Castle, Claife, with its twin lake entrances, dwarfs other Lake District boathouses. It dates from the late 1840s. [Author].

coal proprietor and brick-maker of Dukinfield Lodge, near Ashton-under-Lyne, but on his death in 1825 it was inherited by his infant son Francis Dukinfield Palmer Astley, and the villa was let. Astley junior returned as a young man in or shortly after 1847 before selling in 1859 to Col. George John Miller Ridehalgh (1835-92), who was a founder member of the Windermere Sailing Club inaugurated in January 1860. The club prospered under the patronage of numerous wealthy villa owners and in 1887, the year of Queen Victoria's Golden Jubilee, it acquired the Royal Warrant, becoming known as the Royal Windermere Yacht Club.

Ridehalgh took his boating very seriously at a time when many young amateurs were arguing that real competition required the longstanding reliance upon professional crews to be abandoned. He was also a keen hunter and one-time Master of the Windermere Harriers, who used boats to ferry his dogs up and down the lake. In 1860 Ridehalgh raced *Wave Crest* and *Gazelle*, both qualifying for the 20ft class of yacht, and in 1870 and 1871 he took delivery of *Emerald* and *Britannia* respectively. But he also took pride in having the latest technology at his disposal. In 1859, the same year he acquired Fell Foot, he took delivery of a Clyde-built steamer named *Fairy Queen*, which he made available for prize-giving on race days. From 1863 *Fairy Queen* was lit by an on-board gas-raising plant. *Fairy Queen*'s successor was a sleek iron-hulled screw steamer, also named *Britannia*, at 80ft-long 'probably the grandest and most opulent vessel ever to grace the waters of Windermere'. She was built on the Clyde by T. B. Seath & Co. and shipped in pieces to Lakeside, where she was assembled from late 1878 and launched by Miss Ridehalgh on 24 June 1879. But she was 'quite too large and unwieldy for the lake', and served mainly for the holding of parties.[23]

Ridehalgh's contemporary and fellow enthusiast, William Forwood, noted that he 'constructed a perfect miniature dockyard' at Fell Foot, modifying a substantial stretch of the lake shore as he developed his passion for both sail and steam. The existing boathouse was enlarged slightly to create a more generous and better-lit stone stage along one side. Externally the change registers as no more than a slight asymmetry, as the roof falls to a lower eaves level on the north side, but inside the wall-plate on this side is propped to create a narrow aisle, equipped with a broad shallow recess for storing oars and other equipment. An adjoining store (the building has no water entrance), present by 1859 and probably built by Astley or one of his tenants, was retained. Next to it a wet dock was added, and beyond these Ridehalgh built a large dual-purpose dry boathouse and banqueting room with a boat-repair yard alongside, and a second wet boathouse. The dry boathouse has a chimneypiece dated 1869.

The result of Ridehalgh's efforts was a long line of boathouses and related structures unparalleled among the villa estates of the Lake District (**Fig.**

Fig. 11 The boathouses and related structures at Fell Foot, Staveley-in-Cartmel. The earliest boathouse, probably late eighteenth-century, is on the extreme right. The dry boathouse of 1869 occupies the centre with the boat repair yard set back to its left. [Allison Borden].

11). The centrepiece is the large dry boathouse, which adopts the fashion, then sweeping the nearby resort of Grange-over-Sands, for lintels and other ornament of extravagantly water-worn limestone. The timber-lined interior was lit by gas, generated at a gas plant built to serve the house in 1865, and two remarkable gasoliers remain suspended from the boarded ceiling. Each has ten gas jets radiating horizontally beneath a polished metal globe acting in much the same manner as a night-club glitter-ball; when lit they must have given a striking lustre to regatta or race-day festivities.

Maintaining a fleet of boats was an expensive hobby, requiring frequent outlay. On the north side of the dry boathouse was the working heart of Ridehalgh's operation. Here a slipway allowed boats to be winched out of the water so that maintenance and repair could proceed under cover. The end of the building facing the lake frontage was an open-sided structure supported on cast-iron columns, its workaday purpose softened by the presence of ornate cast-iron spandrels (**Fig. 12**). A wall-mounted jib crane facilitated heavy lifting; natural light and ventilation could be varied using the hinged timber sidings which were suspended from the wall-plates; and light was provided by the gas supply. The concern for such details, paralleled in the structure of the dry boathouse, announces the facilities as something to be shown off, at least among a circle of like-minded enthusiasts.

Fig. 12 Cast-iron column and spandrels on the open-sided section of the Fell Foot covered boatyard, probably of 1869. [Allison Borden].

THE FUTURE OF THE BOATHOUSE

After the First World War the halcyon days of the Edwardian elite proved hard to restore. Many villa owners found themselves struggling with changed economic conditions and sold out. But the popularity of the Lakes as a venue for recreation and sport was undiminished and it was the great pleasure yachts rather than the boathouses that fell out of use. Today the great majority of the boathouses built between 1770 and 1914 survive, though many are under-used by the standards of the nineteenth century and this can lead to inadequate maintenance. Periodic flooding is also a threat. The devastating floods of November 2009 nearly destroyed the attractive 1866 boathouse belonging to Wansfell Holme, while at Fell Foot Colonel Ridehalgh's great dry boathouse has not operated as a tea room for two years. Some seem to be used only desultorily, a small fibreglass rowing boat occupying a space once intended for a prized racing yacht. But a number enable outdoor activity centres in the Lake District to offer tuition in sailing and canoeing, and a few are used by steam-boat enthusiasts, whose slim whispering craft venture forth on still summer days, recalling a lost world. For as long as the English remain enchanted by all things nautical some boathouses at least are assured of a use.

Is boating in the Lake District still a patriotic pursuit? Perhaps not, but the commercial steamers plying the larger lakes are registered by law with the maritime authorities, and so proudly fly the Red Ensign.

Notes

1. Jared Curtis (ed.), *The Fenwick Notes of William Wordsworth*, London, 1993, p. 85.

2. Cumbria Record Office (Kendal), WDRC/8/293.

3. William Wordsworth, *Guide to the Lakes* (5th edn, 1835), ed. Ernest de Sélincourt, Oxford, 1906, p. 63.

4. W.J.B. Owen and Jane Worthington Smyser (eds.), *The Prose Works of William Wordsworth*, 3 vols., Oxford, 1974, vol. II, p. 372.

5. James Clarke, *A Survey of the Lakes of Cumberland, Westmorland, and Lancashire*, London, 1787, p. 23.

6. William Hutchinson, *An Excursion to the Lakes in Westmoreland and Cumberland; with a Tour through part of the Northern Counties in the years 1773 and 1774*, London, 1776, pp. 64, 68-71.

7. Adam Menuge, 'Belle Isle, Windermere, Cumbria', RCHME Historic Building Report, 1997. See also Peter Leach, 'The House with a View in Late Eighteenth-Century England: A Preliminary Inquiry', *Georgian Group Journal*, 16, 2008, pp. 117-31.

8. William Hutchinson. *The History of the County of Cumberland*, 2 vols., Carlisle, 1794, vol. 2, facing p. 167.

9. Joseph Pocklington, *Pocklington's Island*, engraved by H. Ashby, London, 1783; revised 1788, reprinted in Alan Hankinson, *The Regatta Men*, Milnthorpe, 1988, plate 2.

10. A.G. Banks, *H.W. Schneider of Barrow and Bowness*, Kendal, 1984, p. 91.

11. For Crosthwaite, see Peter Brears, 'Commercial Museums of Eighteenth-Century Cumbria: The Crosthwaite, Hutton and Todhunter Collections', *Journal of the History of Collections*, 4:1, 1992, pp. 107-26.

12. Ian Goodall and Simon Taylor, 'Storrs Hall, Windermere, Cumbria', English Heritage Architectural Investigation Reports and Papers B/029/2002. For the extraordinary boathouse projected at Storrs Hall (but not built) by J. M. Gandy in the form of a Greek temple, see Ian Goodall and Margaret Richardson, 'A Recently Discovered Gandy Sketchbook', *Architectural History*, 44, 2001, pp. 45-56; Ian Goodall, 'Storrs Hall, Windermere', *Georgian Group Journal*, 15, 2006, pp. 159-214.

13. I am grateful to Sophia Martin for introducing me to this building, and to Janet Martin for discussing aspects of its background.

14. 'Mr Alderman Carr of York' is identified as the architect in the sale notice published in the *Cumberland Pacquet*, 2 September 1800.

15. *Westmorland Gazette*, 1 August 1840.

16. George H. Pattinson, *The Great Age of Steam on Windermere*, Windermere, 1981, pp. 13-14. For further information on boats and boating in the Lake District the following sources (in addition to those referenced below) have proved particularly useful: Sir William B. Forwood, *Reflections of a Busy Life, being the Reminiscences of a Liverpool Merchant 1840 – 1910*, Liverpool, 1910; Barbara Hall (ed.), *The Royal Windermere Yacht Club 1860-1960*, Altrincham, 1960; and Diana R. Matthews, *Lake Festivals on Windermere*, Windermere, 1982.

17. Adam Menuge & Ian Goodall, 'Wray Castle, Claife, Cumbria', Historic Building Report, 2006.

18. Sir William B. Forwood (ed.), *Windermere and the Royal Windermere Yacht Club*, Kendal, 1905, unpaginated.

19. Wordsworth (note 3), p.63.

20. The history of Fell Foot, unless referenced otherwise, follows Janet Martin, *Fell Foot Park & Garden*, London, 1996. I am grateful to Dr Sarah Rutherford for discussing her recent researches into the designed landscapes both here and at Claife Station, and to Sarah Woodcock for making available photographs of the Fell Foot boathouses and others in the care of the National Trust.

21. *St James's Chronicle*, 19 July 1785.

22. Cumbria Record Office (Kendal), WPR/89/Z 3.

23. Forwood (note 18), unpaginated.

4 Practical yet Artistic:
The Motor House, 1895–1914

JOHN MINNIS

One of the most striking aspects of the introduction of the motor car into England was the speed with which the fledgling industry took off. By 1905, 16,000 cars were on the road, and the whole apparatus of a motor trade existed with new and used car dealers, motor auctions and a trade press. This was only ten years since the first motor show was held in Tunbridge Wells under the auspices of Sir David Salomons, landowner, scientist, inventor and champion of the motor car, mustering some four cars – probably all that existed in England at the time. By 1912, the total number of cars registered in England and Wales had risen to 156,573.[1]

The arrival of the motor car in England in the late 1890s brought in its wake a number of new building types to supply, fuel, service and house the new-fangled and often temperamental machine. At first, existing stables, sheds and workshops were adapted but, within a few years, purpose-built designs to house the car began to emerge.[2] Some of these were on a grand scale, the equivalent of country house stables with accommodation for chauffeurs and mechanics, forges and workshops, reflecting the wealth of early motorists. By the beginning of the Edwardian period, motoring, while still a rich man's hobby, increasingly became taken up by the upper end of the middle class and it is their more modest motor houses that are the focus of this paper. It is based on material gathered for 'The Car Project', a national research project on the impact of the motor car on the built environment and landscape being undertaken by the author and Kathryn Morrison of English Heritage.[3]

WHY WERE MOTOR HOUSES NECESSARY?

Early motor cars, as their alternative name, 'horseless carriages', suggests, shared much in common with their horse-drawn predecessors. Indeed, their bodies were often built by the very same coachbuilders as horse-drawn carriages, with firms such as Barker (founded 1710), Cockshoot (founded 1724) and Hooper (founded 1805) active at the upper end of the market. The bodies, and, in the early examples, the chassis, were largely built of wood and were painted in the traditional coach-builders' manner. This entailed the application of many successive coats of primers, fillers, guide coat, stopping coat, what was described as 'common colour' and 'best colour', followed by hand varnishing. Each coat of paint took a long time to dry and the whole process could easily take twenty days.[4] The result was a finish that was very easily scratched when the car was washed and would suffer badly from exposure to rain or the sun or excessive heat. The varnish would crack, the gloss would go flat and the timber would start to split. Indeed, it was recommended that, on return from each journey, cars were thoroughly washed down, cleaned and dried. The appalling state of much of the road network contributed to this requirement. In addition, early motor cars required a great deal of routine maintenance and it was essential to have somewhere where this could be carried out under cover and where the tools and the prodigious quantity of spare parts needed could be stored.

THE ORIGINS OF THE MOTOR HOUSE

The accommodation was initially referred to as a 'motor house' and this was the term most widely used until 1914 with 'motor stables' as an alternative for the larger complex. 'Garage' tended to be used to describe a public car park and then a place where cars were sold, repaired and maintained. It was certainly used in that sense in 1902 when *The Car Illustrated* stated that '"garage", an unfortunate word borrowed like many of our automobile terms from our friends across the Channel … signifies a motor-car store-house' and went on to use the term to describe parking and repair and maintenance garages.[5] But already the distinction was becoming blurred with Charles Harrison Townsend noting in 1908 that, ' for the home of the car, we very largely use the French word "garage", alternatively with what I think the more desirable English equivalent of "motor house"'.[6] He went on to use 'garage' to mean a public storing place for cars in a paper he gave to the Architectural Association.

When was the first motor house built? It may well have been constructed by Salomons himself at Broomhill, his house near Tunbridge Wells, at about the time he acquired his first motor cars in 1895-6 but there is no documentary evidence to provide a precise date. Certainly, he had already replaced his original motor house by an enlarged version (which still exists) by 1902.[7] There was also a 'motor-garage' for five cars and several motor-tricycles constructed by the Hon. Evelyn Ellis at Datchet, Berkshire, which was in existence by 1900.[8] But both Ellis' and Salomons' motor houses were on a large scale, designed to house numerous vehicles, rather than the smaller structures that are the focus of this paper.

The earliest motoring magazines were uncharacteristically silent on the question of housing cars, the only reference being to a French architect's suggestion that new houses in Paris ought to be fitted up with 'coach-houses for autocars'.[9] The first motor house to be depicted in an English motoring journal was in *The Autocar*, which, in its issue for 7 October 1899, published an interview with Dr W. W. Barrett, a pioneer motorist from Southport in Lancashire.[10] Dr Barrett was one of the first doctors in the north of England to use a car for his rounds instead of a horse and carriage. He acquired his first car, a 5½ horsepower Daimler, in May 1898, and the second, a specially built covered-in Daimler, in December 1898. He was a keen motorist, extolling the virtues of using a car for his work, and was a vice-president of the Southport Automobile Club.

Dr Barrett designed a motor house specially to house the cars, located to the rear of his large late nineteenth-century house at no. 29 Park Crescent, Hesketh Park (**Fig.1**). It was a two-storey building in red brick matching the house and linked to the dining room by a corridor. On the ground floor was the accommodation for the cars with a brick floor laid on concrete. This garage was electrically lit and, like the house, heated by hot water. The doctor was therefore able to go from the warmth of his centrally-heated house to his car without venturing into the cold, an important consideration for someone who might have to travel at all hours in the course of his work. The garage had an engine pit on two levels (two feet and four feet deep) and was fully

Fig. 1 Dr Barrett's motor house, Hesketh Park, Southport, from *The Autocar,* 7 October 1899, and the first to be illustrated in the British motoring press.

equipped with tools and equipment, some of it designed by Dr Barrett. The first floor was occupied by a billiard room and the doctor's workroom, filled with lathes, cutting machines and a circular saw, where he was able to indulge his interest in mechanical matters. The motor house was almost square with a projecting bay to the front. A broad opening with a moulded arch provided the vehicle entrance. The doors were set back behind this so that the projecting bay formed a two-storey porch. While the building was quite plain, corner buttresses to the projecting bay and stone surrounds to the windows provided a few decorative touches.

Although many of the large houses around Hesketh Park have been replaced with blocks of flats since 1945, no. 29 has survived, converted into flats, and with it, the motor house, now also entirely in residential use. The garage doors have been replaced with a window, a door has been inserted into the corridor to give independent access and all windows have been renewed in uPVC, although broadly echoing the appearance of the original timber sashes. Other than this, the motor house is unchanged externally from Dr Barrett's day and is in good condition. It has not proved possible to trace plans so the exact date of construction is unknown (the building replaced what was probably a stable shown on the 1894 edition of the 25" Ordnance Survey map) but it is likely Dr Barrett may have constructed his motor house some time before he obtained his first car in May 1898 and certainly no later.

Fig. 2 1902 motor house, 34 Chantry Road, Moseley, Birmingham, photographed in December 2007. [John Minnis/ English Heritage].

As the earliest purpose-built motor house to be illustrated and described, the Southport building may be the earliest surviving example in England of that very common building type, the domestic garage.

By the early 1900s, more modestly priced cars were appearing and a secondhand market began to grow up. In the more prosperous suburbs of the major cities, motor cars began to take their place as a means of transport. The earliest examples were quite small and, although the more prestigious makes soon grew in size, the most popular cars such as the De Dion Bouton and its many imitators remained relatively small. It was possible therefore for many home owners to simply convert an existing stable. Others built small motor houses beside their dwellings. Sometimes, the two are hard to distinguish, especially as the building of stables continued until around 1910.

In Chantry Road, Moseley in Birmingham, a road of large semi-detached and detached houses built at the end of the nineteenth century, there are many early garages and, through the survival of the building plans register, it has proved possible to date some of them. Some such as that at no. 20 are probably converted from stables as they have a prominent opening, circular in this case, which gave access to the hayloft. No. 34 has a purpose-built motor house of 1902. It is quite shallow, built directly against the house. In style, with its half-timbered gable incorporating a louvred ventilator, it complements the house (**Fig. 2**).

Such early motor houses were put up throughout the country and, as they were solidly constructed of brick, have survived in many cases.

THE PREFABRICATED MOTOR HOUSE

In the nineteenth century, a substantial market had grown up for prefabricated buildings, particularly for export. Numerous firms, of which Boulton & Paul of Norwich was the best known, provided a wide range of timber and corrugated iron buildings for almost every purpose from farm buildings to churches. It became clear that the arrival of the motor car created a new market for their products and prefabricated motor houses started to be advertised about 1903. Often referred to as portable or temporary motor houses, they covered a wide range of styles and prices. In 1903, one was offered by A.G. Quibell of West Green Road, London N., which had gablets and a Venetian window to the side elevations, with a weather vane and circular windows on the doors.[11] The same year, Boulton & Paul was offering an 18ft x 16ft motor house with clapboarding to waist level and half-timbering above for £42. Their range included designs that incorporated an extension of the roof forming a glazed washing shelter and a de luxe model that had a workshop at the rear. More elaborate designs were available including ones specially designed to fit into picturesque garden settings with thatched roofs and

Fig. 3 Boulton & Paul motor house, advertised in *The Car Illustrated*, 3 April 1907.

ornamental brackets supporting a deeply overhanging gable (**Fig. 3**). The word 'artistic' was widely used in advertising the garages. Horizontal clapboarding was a popular feature, being found in two other companies' products. The St John's Timber Co. of Battersea Rise had a design with small paned windows, ornamental bargeboards and a prominent ventilator on the roof ridge while the South Western Timber Co. of Fulham offered a similar design but with a half-hipped gable end and oval windows in the garage doors (**Fig. 4**). Browne & Lilly of Reading, perhaps second in size to Boulton & Paul, offered a similar structure with broadly Arts & Crafts treatment including a gablet and battered corners (**Fig. 5**). The Portable Building Co. of Manchester also offered motor houses with 'rustic-jointed weatherboarding' half way up the exterior walls and half timbering above, the interior fully matchboarded and with corrugated iron roofs, at prices between £21 10s to £75 plus erection charges.[12] One striking example of 1903 came from Sweden, with the Country Gentleman's Association as the British agents.[13] It had particularly elaborate fretted barge boards, ridge board and ventilator and was well protected against damp and fire with sheets of damp-proof felt and asbestos sandwiched between two or three layers of wood. It was expected that such structures should not detract

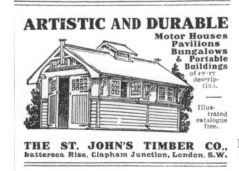

Fig. 4 St John's Timber Co. motor house, 1912, from *The Motor*, 3 December 1912.

from the appearance of the house. Being of timber construction, prefabricated motor houses have been subject to decay if not regularly painted and the only one surviving into recent years to be traced so far is a 1914 Browne & Lilly example, removed from Hadley Wood, Barnet – where it was under threat of demolition – to Wales by the motoring historian, Michael Worthington-Williams, for his own use.[14]

THE PETROL STORE

In the days before petrol was easily obtainable, motorists needed to maintain adequate fuel supplies themselves and the storage of the volatile liquid presented problems. It was normally sold in two-gallon tins which were refilled each time motorists visited their suppliers. The storage of the petrol was recommended to be in a separate fireproof building away from the car. Although this would usually have been constructed of brick, Boulton & Paul advertised steel-framed fireproof buildings for the storage of petrol.[15] A surviving petrol store has been identified at Ashton Wold, Northamptonshire. It has vents both below the eaves and low down (petrol vapour being heavier than air and accumulated near the floor of a building), a lowered floor that could be filled with sand to absorb spillages, and slate shelves on iron supports to reduce fire risk. All these precautions, however, were negated to some extent by the reed-thatched roof of the store, enabling it to harmonise with other estate buildings.

Fig. 5 Browne & Lilly's 'Artistic Motor House', advertised in *The Motor*, 22 October 1912.

E. KEYNES PURCHASE AND HIS DESIGNS

The motoring journals and the numerous practical motoring manuals that were published from the turn of the century were full of advice for the potential motor house builder. The earliest of these articles, published in the first issue of *The Car Illustrated* in 1902, was by E. Keynes Purchase, a highly successful commercial architect. Keynes Purchase was 'honorary architect' to what became the Royal Automobile Club and was involved in the design of the club's premises in Pall Mall. He was to produce many similar schemes for motor houses until well into the 1920s. He recommended a straight drive in and, ideally, brick rather than wood or corrugated iron construction. Cement floors with a fall to one end were best and it was important not to have a drain for this could clog up with oil and, more seriously, harbour petrol vapours leading to the risk of explosion. Light and ventilation were the most important factors with blinds or shutters to keep the sun off the fragile paintwork, top lighting if possible and electricity for artificial light. Heating, if any, should be by hot water pipes. Unlike later writers, Keynes Purchase recommended the inspection pit with its wooden cover be placed outside the building under the glass roof of the washing shelter Inside, some sort of arrangement of pulleys on runners or a hoist was essential to enable the removal of the car's body or its engine, which could then be lifted to a work bench at the rear of the garage (**Fig. 6**).[16]

As cars developed, so too did Keynes Purchase's views as to what was required in the ideal garage. In the one he built at his own home around 1909 in Morden, Surrey, he used cement blocks cast on site for the walls on a concrete base. He dismissed top lights as being too likely to leak and lighted the garage by casement windows on either side: he abandoned the pit because it was so seldom needed, preferring instead to raise the car off the ground, and he carried out car washing inside the garage, rather than under an open-sided glass shelter. The draught from the open garage doors and the side windows was sufficient to dry off the car.[17]

A MOTOR HOUSE FOR TWO CARS

Fig. 6 A motor house for two cars with a washing shelter and external pit. Design by E. Keynes Purchase published in *The Car Illustrated*, 4 June 1902.

He set out his views in greater detail in his chapter 'The Housing of a Car' in the *RAC Year Book* for 1909. He warned of the need to check local authority by-laws as these varied considerably throughout the country, some councils insisting that garages had to be fire-proof, or banning them altogether if they adjoined houses, or setting minimum distances between garage and house. Space for turning the car was important and, if space was available, it was an advantage to have doors at each end of the garage, so that the car could be driven through to turn or wash it. In suburban areas, it was felt that washing the car was something one did in the privacy of one's back garden rather than in front of the garage where it was visible to all who passed. Lighting and heating were considered with, unsurprisingly, the motorist being warned against naked lights and open fires in the motor house. Electricity was recommended for lighting with a movable hand lamp for carrying out inspections and stoves or hot water pipes for heating.[18]

THE MOTOR HOUSE AND THE ARCHITECT

The architectural profession seems to have regarded the motor car as unworthy of its attention, certainly as far as writing about the subject was concerned. The pre-1914 architectural journals are almost devoid of any references to any type of building catering for the car. Yet architects were quite prepared to design suitable buildings if commissioned, among them garages and showrooms by several notable provincial firms. Some of the finest architects in the country, among them Lutyens, Barry Parker and Edgar Wood, at the top end of the market, designed motor houses for their wealthy clients. But a cloud of silence hangs over all this work, as though it was not quite the proper thing. Why is this? One would have thought it a good thing to be associated with something so fashionable, so redolent of wealth, luxury and modernity, as the motor car. Perhaps an element of snobbery towards machinery, associated with 'trade', remained, which precluded too close an identification with designing for the motor. In a world where designing a church was held to be the highest point of architectural endeavour, housing a car ranked near the bottom of the hierarchical scale.

Other than Keynes Purchase, the only other architects to have written on or discussed the question in the architectural press are two who addressed the Architectural Association on the subject, the first, the secretary of its Discussion Section, M. G. Pechell in 1906 and the second, the prominent Arts and Crafts architect, Charles Harrison Townsend in 1908.[19] What did they consider were the basic requirements of a successful motor house?

The first factor to be considered was the size of the motor house which had to be large enough to accommodate the car. In particular it should be long enough for any car that the owner might have in the future, it should be

BEFORE
CONVERSION

AFTER
CONVERSION

Fig. 7 Captain Bowman–Manifold's conversion of a conservatory into a motor house from *The Car Illustrated,* 18 June 1902.

wide enough to enable the doors to be opened and high enough to allow a spare tyre or two to be carried on the roof of the car.

The walls should be faced with glazed bricks or tiles so they could be washed down, the junction of the walls with the floor should be coved to avoid the accumulation of dirt. Air gratings should be placed low down to expel petrol fumes which are heavier than air. Drains should be open, half-round channels rather than underground pipes to prevent the build-up of explosive gases. Heating the garage was essential as the motor house 'cannot be too dry'.

By 1908, the necessity of a pit was not considered to be as great as it had been because car manufacturers were making the mechanical parts more accessible. If a pit was considered essential, it should be 6ft by 3ft by 4ft 6 in. deep. Access should be with wooden steps and ideally it, like the garage should be lined with a washable surface and covered by 2in. thick boards when not in use.

A covered washing space outside the motor house was essential and sometimes it covered an exterior pit. The covering usually took the form of an iron and glass canopy and very few have survived.[20]

The architectural form taken by the motor house was a subject of discussion which favoured the newer term 'garage': 'The country garages now being erected looked like stables, which they were not, and the town garages looked like anything from a restaurant to a private house … an entirely new development like motor cars must bring in its train a new form of architecture'.[21]

Other writers in the motoring journals emphasised the importance of adequate lighting, necessary when cars required constant adjustment, frequent lubrication and repair. Also desirable was the removal of the workshop with its machine tools to a separate room and, unlike Keynes Purchase, they reiterated the importance of the pit – 'when a pit is wanted, it is wanted badly'.[22] One ideal garage, although termed a 'small motor-house', ambitiously included an apartment for 'creative' work where the technical library was kept, where the accounts for the car were maintained and where tours could be mapped out.

> In this way the man who cares for his car in the true sense will show that care in the very architecture of his garage and in the manner of its furnishing. He will build for his car with all the taste and sympathy that was displayed in the building or selection of his own home. The design as a whole will not be so much like a stable and coach-house as like a studio or an atelier.[23]

Perhaps the imaginary garage depicted in **Fig. 9** was for just such a man.

DIFFERING APPROACHES TO HOUSING THE CAR

In many cases, early motorists were interested in cars, not primarily as a means of transport, but as an end in themselves. Engineering was their hobby.

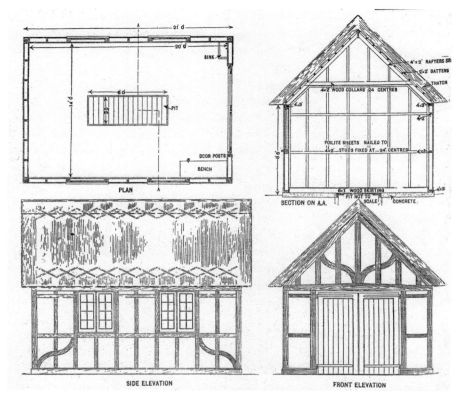

Fig. 8 A 1914 motor house built in Warlingham, Surrey, of Poilite asbestos sheeting, from *The Autocar,* 10 January 1914.

Leonard Williamson, a trained electrical engineer, is one such example and, in an interview with him, *The Car Illustrated* noted that 'his interest in the mechanical side is greater than his interest in driving'.[24] In five and a half years as a motorist, he had owned eighteen machines. At his home at no. 28 Albert Road, Southport, he had a comprehensive workshop with numerous power tools and, in the grounds of the house, a circular test track with sharp curves banked up on which he had achieved a maximum of 25 miles per hour.

Ingenious solutions as to what to do with the motor house proliferated. One in Surrey was disguised as a pavilion on a tennis lawn, complete with a verandah containing a bench facing the lawn, and a darkroom catering for another of the owner's interests.[25] At Tunbridge Wells, in 1909, Elliott Alves used the falling land behind his house to conceal within his garden a garage for three cars, hewn out of solid sandstone below a conservatory. The garage is still used today, retaining the ebonised tile surface of its courtyard although the conservatory and chauffeur's dressing room below it have gone.[26] Converting the conservatory was itself seen as an ideal solution by Captain M. Bowman-Manifold; it had drainage, ventilation and heating and while it needed 'stout brown paper' affixed to the glass roof to keep down the effect of the sun, it was done 'without seriously interfering with its floral utility' (**Fig. 7**).[27]

After 1910, the motor house became less imposing with examples constructed of asbestos panels, 'the latest substitute for brick', or corrugated iron, as well as wood being advertised by W.H. Knight of Bromley Common in 1912 (**Fig. 8**).[28] From around this date, there was a vogue for a new type of car aimed at those with much less to spend, the cyclecar, which, as its name suggests, was a somewhat spindly affair, very lightly constructed with cycle type wheels and accommodating one or two people, generally in extreme

THE ENTHUSIAST.

Fig.9 A cartoon depicting a motoring enthusiast ignoring his long-suffering wife's wish for him to join her and her friends in their game of tennis as he happily works on his lathe. It is interesting in that it gives an idea of the sort of machinery expected in a well-equipped motor house – a lathe, a power hacksaw, a vertical drill, all probably powered by electricity, together with an electrical testing board. The effective lighting is also apparent, with three bulbs above the machinery, roof lights and glazing above the door. The valuable lamps have been removed from the car and stored inside the garage. Drawing by John Bryan (better known in later life as Bryan de Grineau), in *The Motor,* 26 July 1910.

discomfort. These cars were small and some of the tandem type, where the passenger sat behind the driver, could be driven through a front garden gate. They needed no more than11ft by 6ft 6in. to accommodate them and garages began to be advertised, having more in common in many cases with a garden shed than the ornate motor houses.[29]

In 1906, houses on the Hale Estate, Edgware, Middlesex were advertised as 'having room for motor' and motor houses were included in some speculatively built houses in the London area from about 1912.[30] But these were very much the exception and motor owners were generally left to fend for themselves in the provision of accommodation for their cars.

In England, the motor car was still seen as something to be kept at arms length from the house and, not withstanding Dr Barrett's heated passage from dining room to garage, attempts to integrate the housing of the motor car with that of its owner remained rare. In France, however, integral garages began to appear relatively early and *The Car Illustrated* gave examples, chiefly located on the ground or basement floors of three-and four-storey houses, and berated the conservative English for their failure to do likewise.[31] Perhaps the English were less prepared to accept the smell of petrol fumes wafting through the house or were more concerned about fire risk. Alternatively, perhaps England was a little behind those countries where motoring had gained ground earlier. Two accounts of garage design, one French, the other American, include some attractive structures of considerable architectural elaboration and many of the ground plans include turntables, something rarely seen in contemporary English domestic garage descriptions.[32] Overall, however, the motor house in America seems to have developed along similar lines as that in England, with the same mixture of converted stables, purpose-built or prefabricated motor houses and elaborate structures with accommodation for chauffeurs, together with the use of large public garages in the cities.[33]

THE MOTOR HOUSE TODAY

While a number of examples of pre-1914 motor houses have been identified during the course of fieldwork for the Car Project, there must be many more survivors in existence. The greatest threat to them today is that they are often not large enough to take the width of modern cars, whose size, particularly with the increasing popularity of 4x4 vehicles and people carriers, has grown appreciably in recent years. Any upper middle class residential area where there are reasonably large gaps between the houses to provide sufficient room to insert a motor house is worth exploring and should yield up a number of these well-built and substantial structures. If this is combined with research, using building control plans in local record offices or archives, it should prove possible to date some of them or identify additional potential survivals.

ACKNOWLEDGEMENT

Much of the research for this paper was carried out in motoring journals held in the splendid library of the Veteran Car Club of Great Britain, housed at its headquarters in Ashwell, Hertfordshire, and I would like to thank the club and its Hon. Librarian, Simon Moss, for help and encouragement freely given.

Notes

1. *The Car Illustrated*, 11 December 1912, pp. 167–8.

2. The history of motor houses has been examined in three articles: William Boddy, 'Garages fit for Motor Cars', *The Veteran and Vintage Magazine*, September 1965, pp. 8–9, 32; Treve Rosoman, 'The Motor House', *Traditional Homes*, March 1987, pp. 11–16; Michael Worthington-Williams, 'The Motor House', *The Automobile*, December 2001, pp. 48–51.

3. The larger motor stables will be considered in the book that will result from the project.

4. See Nick Walker, *A-Z British Coachbuilders 1919-1960*, Beaworthy, 2007, which, although relating to the period following World War One, describes coach building methods that had changed little since the inception of the motor car.

5. *The Car Illustrated*, 28 May 1902, p. 8.

6. *The Builder*, 15 February 1908, p. 175.

7. The motor stable was described in detail and illustrated in David Salomons, 'The Motor Stable and its management' in Alfred C. Harmsworth (ed.), *Motors and Motor-driving*, London, 1902. Further description and analysis is in John Minnis, *Sir David Salomons' Motor Stables, Broomhill, Southborough, Tunbridge Wells, Kent*, English Heritage Research Department Report Series no. 7-2009, available as a download from the English Heritage website.

8. *The Motor-Car Journal*, 16 March 1900, pp. 17, 19.

9. *The Autocar*, 6 June 1896, p. 379.

10. Ibid., 7 October 1899, pp. 897–9.

11. *The Motor*, 4 March 1903, advertising supplement.

12. Portable Building Co. catalogue, n.d., *c.*1909.

13. *Motoring Illustrated*, 16 May 1903, p. 328.

14. Mr Worthington-Williams later moved house and, most regrettably, although it had been listed, the motor house was demolished some years ago by a subsequent owner of the property.

15. *The Car Illustrated*, 20 December 1905, p. 193.

16. E. Keynes Purchase, 'Motor Houses', *The Car Illustrated*, 28 May 1902, pp. 7–8.

17. *The Motor*, 2 March 1909, p. 181.

18. E. Keynes Purchase, 'The Housing of a Car', *R.A.C. Year Book*, 1909, pp. 318–23.

19. *The Builder*, 27 October 1906, pp. 483–4, 15 February 1908, pp. 175–83

20. Although built on a much larger scale, an example of one of these iron and glass structures may be seen at the royal garage at Sandringham House.

21. *The Builder*, 15 February 1908, p. 182.

22. *The Motor*, 9 March 1909, pp. 203–4.

23. Ibid., 28 May 1912, p. 737.

24. *The Car Illustrated*, 22 October 1902, p. 280.

25. *Motoring Illustrated*, 20 September 1902, p. 68.

26. *The Car Illustrated*, 10 February 1909, pp. 565-7.

27. Ibid., 18 June 1902, p. 120.

28. *The Motor*, 23 January 1912, supplement, ix. Asbestos was evidently still a novelty two years later as a garage in Warlingham, Surrey, constructed of Poilite, an asbestos material, was featured in *The Autocar*, 10 January 1914, p. 48. Its fireproofing was somewhat compromised by the panel gaps being covered by deal slats in imitation of half timbering and the thatched roof.

29. The requirements for cyclecars are dealt with in 'Cheaper housing for the cyclecar', *The Cyclecar*, 25 December 1912, pp.133-4.

30. Alan A. Jackson, *The Middle Classes 1900-1950*, Nairn, 1991, p. 108.

31. *The Car Illustrated*, 23 July 1913, p. 369.

32. 'Les Garages à la campagne', *La Vie Automobile*, 22 July 1911, pp. 453-5, 'Private garages and Repairs', *Cyclopedia of Automobile Engineering*, Chicago, 1913, pp. 211-34.

33. Leslie G. Goat, 'Housing the Horseless Carriage: America's Early Private Garages', *Perspectives in Vernacular Architecture*, 3, 1989, pp. 62-72.

5 'Where Shall She Live?': Housing the New Working Woman in Late Victorian and Edwardian London

EMILY GEE

'The streets were full of young women just going to business. In the free life of to-day, when so many women earn their own living, often away from their homes, how slight an accident may shipwreck a life! We make charts of our coasts, we know each shoal, we bell-buoy our sand-banks, we build warning lighthouses, and we make safe harbours. But probably the lives lost on our coasts are not a tithe of the lives – the souls – lost on our streets'. [1]

'Are the streets of our great cities as safe as our shores?' [2]

Turning lighthouses into hostels – this maritime metaphor was the rallying cry of the tireless social reformer and campaigner for working women's housing, Mary Higgs. Initially concerned with destitute women, the Oldham-based Higgs began her social investigations in northern cities, staying undercover in a number of common lodging houses, workhouse tramp wards and municipal lodgings. In 1910 she published her landmark work, *Where Shall She Live? The Homelessness of the Woman Worker* for the National Association for Women's Lodging-Homes (NAWLH). This polemic marked a shift: it discussed all housing options for women, but concentrated on that which Higgs and many others thought was most needed: accommodation for the growing number of women in the lower-earning professions and clerical jobs. Higgs and the NAWLH argued that sound and numerous hostels ('lighthouses'), were needed to save the new working woman from lodging houses of dubious repute amidst the tumultuous waves of urban life.

WOMEN IN THE WORKPLACE

The advancement of women as workers outside the home was a major social and economic development of the late nineteenth and early twentieth centuries. About one quarter of Edwardian women were engaged in work – which was not much higher than the statistic from half a century before – but the *kinds* of work they were doing were changing considerably (**Fig. 1**).

Between 1861 and 1911, the number of women clerical workers increased dramatically from 279 to 124,000.[3] In 1901 still only 1.6 per cent of women were employed in office work but by 1921 this had risen to 15.1 per cent – a sevenfold increase in twenty years.[4] As they came to work as clerks, nurses, shop assistants and typists, they were drawn to urban centres and away from traditional home arrangements.

Such later-nineteenth-century inventions as the telephone and the typewriter resulted in new commercial and communication buildings, which were staffed by a new influx of working women. By 1902, when the first large telephone exchange opened in London, 31 per cent of women were engaged in industrial and domestic employment, nearly four per cent employed as stenographers, typists, secretaries, book-keepers and cashiers.[5] This burgeoning community of working women had a considerable presence in Edwardian London, which created a major spatial and moral challenge. The big question for the single working woman was: where shall she live?

INSTITUTIONS EMERGE TO HOUSE WORKING WOMEN AND GIRLS

The matter was clearly of great concern and many groups had their own solutions and campaigns. The work of assisting women and girls in urban areas was taken up by a number of effective Christian organisations founded in the nineteenth century. These included the Church Army, the Salvation Army, the Young Women's Christian Association (YWCA) and the Girls' Friendly Society (GFS), all initially focussed on working-class women. The earliest project for poorer women was an imaginative conversion of a London town house to accommodate 57 women by the Society for Improving the Condition of the Labouring Classes (SICLC). Bedrooms and parlours were turned into corridors with cubicles, all within the existing structure of the house. A generation later, this work was promoted by the Homes for Working

Fig. 1 A typical scene of Edwardian women in clerical work in the Enquiry Department at the International Correspondence School, London 1909. [English Heritage/NMR].

Girls (HWG) in London, established in 1878 by John Shrimpton. The HWG's Smithfield branch adopted an eighteenth-century house and converted it around 1880 to house 35 women in cubicle lodgings much in the way that the SICLC house had done.

The Soho Club, founded by Maude Stanley in 1884 on Greek Street, housed 30 working women, most of whom were described as 'comfortable', and therefore it was not a rescue home except for in a few cases. However, the campaigning literature played to late-Victorian sensibilities and reported that 'a great many girls were known to have been preserved from danger whilst in London by living in the home, a great many have had excellent places found for them, either in business or in service … But there must be, we grieve to say, the other side of the picture. Some have chosen and followed pleasure along, and have yielded to temptation, and we know not where they are.'[6]

All of these housing options were often quite small, and the membership requirements, religious undertones and class distinctions meant they were not considered suitable for all. Moreover, there were simply not enough. An 1883 pamphlet of the Homes for Working Girls estimated that 800,000 women in England supported themselves through paid work, and that about 320,000 of these were in London. This vast number of women needed reasonable options in which to live.

LATE-NINETEENTH-CENTURY MIDDLE CLASS LADIES' DWELLINGS

A model was established by residential schemes for middle class women of the 1880s and 1890s when a flurry of essays highlighted the emerging need. Women campaigned in their journals for a 'Castle in the Air', described in *Work and Leisure* (1888) as 'a happy and safe dwelling for some hundred of more ladies who are proud to know and style themselves 'Working Bees' in this great busy hive of London'.[7] This ideal dwelling house was to have a variety of room options (from cubicles to apartments), a restaurant, common rooms and various services, because the need for 'wholesome and cheap lodging is so greatly felt by unprotected women of all ranks'.[8] These developments were encouraged by new limited dividend companies whose businesslike approach to developing lodgings attracted women investors and residents alike. Although these schemes had a sound social principle, any perception of charity would have counteracted the spirit of independence that women associated with their new building type. It was this savvy financial rigour that appealed to late Victorian and Edwardian women who took pride in gaining their financial independence.

An early project was Sloane Gardens House, built for the Ladies' Associated Dwellings Company and opened in 1888 at 52 Lower Sloane Street (**Fig. 2**).

Fig. 2 Sloane Gardens House opened in 1888 to house 150 single women in an elegant and richly-ornamented building that aligned it architecturally with wealthy mansion blocks in the area. [Geoff Brandwood].

It accommodated about 150 women mostly in single bed-sitting rooms (an arrangement where the bedroom could be screened off from a living room in essentially one space) but also in cubicles on the upper floors. The shops along the ground floor sold goods from 'millinery to farm or garden produce'. Some of the goods were made by the women residents, and the serviced building included a library, music room and communal dining room. Contemporary comment recorded that 'while retaining their entire independence, the ladies may live with greater comfort and economy than in lodging houses of the ordinary type'. [9] Its claims to 'economy' were overrated, however, as the building was criticised in *Work and Leisure* the year after opening as being 'a handsome, airy and well-appointed establishment ...[but] it does not afford what was at first proposed – board and lodging within the means of working gentlewomen with no fixed income.'[10]

A similar project was opened the following year, 1889, in Bloomsbury: the Chenies Street Chambers built for the Ladies' Residential Chambers Company Ltd. It was designed by J.M. Brydon, an architect who favoured the Queen Anne style for his buildings for women, such as the Elizabeth Garrett Anderson Hospital on the Euston Road. This was a satisfactory style for these large-scale residential buildings and the gables, sash windows and red brick walls and dormers (sadly the roofline was much altered after wartime bombing), all suggested a comforting domestic environment. These chambers catered for middle- and upper-class women working as doctors, artists and music teachers, who lived in individual bed-sitting rooms, with a shared dining room, which ensured the requisite privacy and decorum of their social class.

This company's second project was the York Street Chambers, designed by Eustace Balfour and Thackeray Turner in 1892. This was not, at first glance, dissimilar to other mansion blocks in Marylebone although a stone plaque announced it as being exclusively for ladies. The 50 residents had a choice of flats (bedrooms with separate sitting rooms) or bed-sitting rooms, which were both relatively commodious arrangements. The basement had both private and large communal dining rooms as well as servants' rooms ostensibly providing housing for another less visible class of working women. These layouts suited an emerging class of professional women with a genteel balance of private accommodation that allowed for respectability and independence also with some communal spaces that fostered networking, support and camaraderie. Indeed the first women members of the RIBA, sisters Ethel and Bessie Charles, ran their architectural practice from here.[11]

MUNICIPAL EFFORTS TO HOUSE WORKING WOMEN AND MEN

While the charitable and business-minded institutions mentioned so far were progressive, municipal provision for women was painfully slow. The aspiration that local authorities would provide safe and comfortable lodgings was at the heart of the first major campaign of the philanthropists who concerned themselves with the housing of women. Higgs and her fellow advocates hoped that the London County Council would have heeded their advice in the capital, but despite the LCC's repeated attempts from 1897 to build a municipal women's lodging house, it was not successful. The LCC investigated the need for such lodgings and even prepared architectural plans, but due to the requirement for such schemes to be financially self-sufficient, and through government's repeated disapproval, the plans were never realised.

The LCC considered several sites in central London, such as this proposal of 1905 on Parker Street near Drury Lane (**Fig. 3**). The partnership of Davis and Emmanuel designed a four-storey women's common lodging house with accommodation for 50 women in a series of cubicles squeezed into every corner of the plan. Unlike the contemporary and non-municipal hostels that we will examine next, this plan gave very little space to communal areas suggesting that it was for hard-working working-class women who would simply lodge here between long days working at London's factories and laundries. Ever conscious of class distinctions, the LCC's housing manager concluded in 1901 that, considering the two classes of employment for women (clerks, typists, bookbinders; and laundresses, tailoresses and those employed in factories), 'it appears to me desirable that both these classes should, if possible,

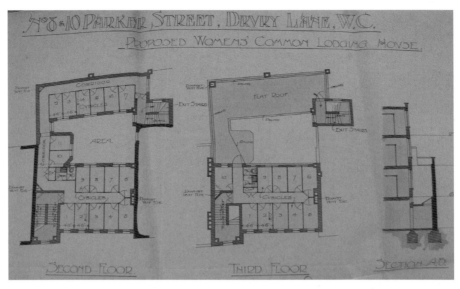

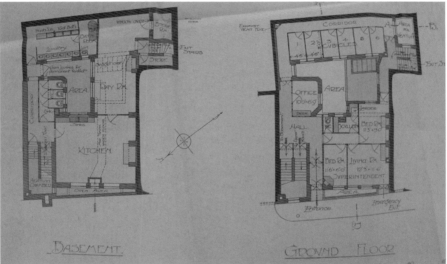

Figs. 3a–b Proposed LCC Women's Common Lodging House, Parker Street, dated 31 October 1905. There was unusually no common sitting room, but a large kitchen and a small day-room in the basement as well as 50 cubicles.
[London Metropolitan Archives, GLC/AR/BR/22/027856].

have provision made for them in a lodging house. But I am of the opinion that this could not be done in one and the same house unless it was so constructed as to be entirely divided and entered from separate streets.'[12]

Despite the thoughtfully worked-out plans, it was deemed impossible to build a house of the necessary size and type that would be economically self-supporting. Men's projects had the same government requirement of self-sufficiency, but given their much greater scale and higher men's wages, this was easier to meet.

In 1910, the LCC's Medical Officer re-visited the failed aspiration for a municipal lodging house. He identified over 2,000 beds across London in authorised common lodging houses for women and revealed that the real need was amongst educated, low-wage earning women, not women of 'irregular and often immoral life' or factory girls.[13] However, factory workers were too poor to afford and sustain a municipal housing project, and conversely, poor middle-class women did not fit into the LCC's aims of housing the destitute. Consequently, the LCC's efforts were frozen and both classes of working women were left out.

This contrasted dramatically with the provision for men, for whom three monumental LCC lodging houses were built between 1892 and 1906. The first, also on Parker Street, was designed in 1892 by Gibson and Russell. As built, Parker Street House was a much-diminished design, but the main door survives with the iron name in the fanlight. 320 men were housed in four highly-ventilated classes of accommodation from single beds to the 'Glasgow method' where one bed was stacked on top of another with entry from cubicles on opposite sites. The LCC's next project was the architecturally superior Carrington House, designed in 1903 by the skilful in-house architectural team. The six-storey Carrington House had a stripped down Arts and Crafts styling with spare detailing and distinctive end pavilions. This lodging house accommodated over 800 men and featured a large smoking room, a well-lit reading room with three fireplaces, a feet-washing room, boot-brushing room, a tailor and a boot-maker's shop. The LCC was encouraging men into work and helping them to remain, or become, presentable for employment.

The LCC's three lodging houses for men were supplemented by the six Rowton Houses built between 1892 and 1905 by the mighty philanthropist Lord Rowton. Altogether these lodging houses, or 'working men's hotels', provided over 7,000 beds for the capital's labouring men. The Rowton Houses are well known as a building type, due to their colossal presence with tiny windows in vast red brick walls with spare, landmark corner towers, most designed by the Edwardian architect of Tube stations and institutions, Harry M. Measures. The last Rowton House to be built, in Camden Town, accommodated over 1,000 men (**Fig. 4**). While entirely secular, these establishments encouraged redemptive, improving activity with large reading rooms and further employment-inducing services.

In contrast to this major municipal and philanthropic provision for men,

Fig. 4 Camden Town Rowton House, Arlington Street opened in 1905. George Orwell, on his tramps through London recorded in *Down and Out in Paris and London* of 1933, p. 133, commented that 'the Rowton Houses really are magnificent … splendid buildings.' [M.J. Shaw].

emerging women's needs were met through alternative philanthropic and entrepreneurial measures: the Edwardian hostels that developed from 1900 as a hybrid of ladies' chambers and the working men's hotels. Many British towns and cities managed to fulfil their duty for municipal housing for women long before London did. Glasgow's first municipal women's lodging house was built in 1872 with room for 125 cheaply-let beds and Cardiff provided a women's hostel from 1911. England's municipal exemplar, however, was Manchester, which opened the first purpose-built model lodging house for women along modern lines in 1910. Ashton House, designed by the City Architect, H.R.Price, catered for 222 women, with beds in a series of dormitories with cubicles (**Fig. 5**). The paired narrow sash windows and the plain upper and side elevations hinted at the building's function, and its scale and name suggested an institutional use, but this was a building of quality in its design and materials and Manchester was clearly proud of its civic duty.

THE LITERARY HEROINE AND HER ACCOMMODATION

Before the women's hostel developed as a building type, the most common arrangement for the new working woman in the city was in lodgings, such as the home of a former family servant, a professional landlady, or a family home.

Mary Erle and Jenny Ingram, two characters from novels, typified middle class young women working in London and the different housing options available to them. The heroine of Ella Hepworth Dixon's *The Story of a Modern Woman*, first published in 1894, began her life in a 'tall London house' in Harley Street, but after the death of her father, Mary Erle shifted her pursuits from art to journalism and moved to furnished rooms in Bulstrode Street.

The description of her accommodation paints a characteristic picture of a lodging woman's existence in the late-Victorian period: she ascended 'from the narrow passage … of which the varnished marble paper, as well as the grained staircase and stiff patterned oil-cloth were worn and stained with age … to her own domain, which consisted of two rooms. In the little bed-room, giving onto a grimy back yard, there was a small iron bed with starved-looking pillows, a washing apparatus … two chairs and a chest of drawers in imitation grained wood, with white china handles'.[14] While a number of nineteenth-century ladies' chambers were built by this date, the substantive hostels where Mary could have lodged in basic but comfortable accommodation with other journalists and clerks had not yet emerged.

A decade later, the determined protagonist of *The Ambitions of Jenny Ingram*, published in 1907, arrived in London from rural Wales to pursue a career in journalism. Jenny also initially lodged with a family, in Bloomsbury, but two years later, the professionally-rejected young woman was: 'living in one room in a large barrack-like building that was let out to many women who were mostly engaged, as she was, in trying to earn an existence.'[15] Exhausted and downtrodden, Jenny ventured into the heart of London's East End desperate to finish her piece on the Whitechapel settlement, but she collapsed on the steps of a philanthropic women's home. The nuns who ran this charitable haven found anonymous Jenny and were clear 'that she was no East End factory girl'; even though she was poor from lack of work, her apparent social class and respectability meant Jenny belonged in the reputable – if barrack-like – hostels of the West End and out of the refuges of the East End. While the author

Fig. 5 Ashton House, Corporation Street, Manchester, opened in 1910 as England's first municipal lodging house for women. A sober yet well-articulated Arts and Crafts Grade II-listed building with subtle castellation and the name picked out in stylish lettering. [Mark Watson].

Fig. 6 Brabazon House in Westminster, opened in 1902. R.S. Ayling concentrated the detail on the façade whereas the architectural effect of the densely-packed rooms and cubicles behind was fairly institutional. [Author].

was disparaging about the modern hostels, this melodrama illustrates the new housing options for single working women in Edwardian London.

EDWARDIAN WORKING WOMEN'S HOSTELS

As had been the case with the residential chambers for middle-class women in the 1880s and 1890s, many of the new hostels favoured limited dividend companies for their businesslike, rather than overtly charitable, approach. These companies did deploy emotive language, and the opportunity to save women from peril was an argument of their capital campaigns; however they were sensible investment opportunities, not philanthropy, and those hostels that achieved self-sufficiency with a 4 per cent return for investors were much lauded.

One of the first was Brabazon House on the Vauxhall Bridge Road in Pimlico (**Fig. 6**). It opened in 1902 under the patronage of the Brabazon House Company Ltd and was designed by R.Stephen Ayling. The company was a philanthropic endeavour of Lady Brabazon, the countess of Meath and an esteemed group of trustees. The company appealed for investors by promising a 'suitable' return on capital invested, but also 'great satisfaction in the knowledge that thereby help is given to a number of gentlewomen working in London in difficult and sometimes dangerous conditions.'[16]

This was the first of five hostels that Ayling designed between 1902 and 1914, which provided 438 beds for single working women and earned him membership of the Southern Committee of the NAWLH. Ayling's RIBA obituary pointed out that he specialised in two building types: the rather odd juxtaposition of abattoirs and housing for 'better-class working girls.'[17] His architectural challenge in designing these hostels was to economically house around 100 women in a homely building that also nodded to the grandeur of the patrons, and was generous in its communal rooms while keeping private quarters to a minimum. *The Builder* featured the hostel with a full-page illustration of Ayling's considered composition, however, behind the grand description and title ('Lady Brabazon's Home for Gentlewomen') that might have likened it to the York Street Chambers, this hostel was clearly intended for less well-off women; half the accommodation was in cubicles instead of the roomier bed-sitting rooms of the earlier chambers. Furthermore, Brabazon House had ample shared social rooms: two ground-floor sitting rooms with fireplaces, cornices and large windows and a basement dining room; by comparison, the only shared facility at York Street ladies' chambers was the dining room (**Fig. 7**). When it opened, Brabazon House was celebrated as the first building of its kind in London, a claim that referred to it catering for a large number of lower-middle-class women while being of quality design, appearance and associations.

The second project of the Brabazon House Company was the much larger Hopkinson House, built on the other side of Vauxhall Bridge Road in 1905 to accommodate 120 women in cubicles and bedrooms. Also designed by Ayling, it was illustrated in the *Building News* as 'Hopkinson House, Residence for Ladies'. This hostel was half as big again as Brabazon House and it held a more prominent position on the Pimlico thoroughfare, marked by a corner tower with lead-domed roof, and running back to the leafy Vincent Square behind.

Lessons learned from Brabazon House led to internal improvements at Hopkinson House, such as the enlargement of the main sitting room and the provision of two further sitting rooms on the first floor. The basement housed the dining room, the servants' bedrooms, a small photographic room and the bicycle store, possibly the earliest provision of this useful feature in a women's hostel. On the upper floors were the cubicles and bedrooms, and nurse's and sick rooms for 'sudden or infectious illness', which must have been a very grave concern in this high density housing.[18] All modern conveniences were provided: there were three baths, lavatories and a water closet on each of the upper floors, electricity throughout, and bedrooms were fitted with

Fig. 7 Brabazon House, women dining in the basement dining room. An illustration of 'A London Home for Lady-Clerks' in *The Girl's Own Paper* (n.d., 1902).

metered gas fires, which could boil a kettle, to enable a degree of catering independence.

Similar projects were promoted by the YWCA which had 25 homes and hostels in London by the end of the nineteenth century. Its first major purpose-built hostel was Ames House and Restaurant at 44 Mortimer Street, opened in 1904. The eminent architect Beresford Pite designed the stylish corner building with his characteristic Arts-and-Crafts-infused Mannerism. Pite helped to define the plan of the new building type: it housed 97 women in cubicles and bedrooms (the same sized footprint differentiated by the thickness of the partitions) and featured a small shared sitting room, a large 'public room', a residents' dining room (each of these with fireplaces) and an office for tending to fees and other matters (**Fig. 8**). The ground floor plan was largely given over to other uses such as four shops, which helped to fund the enterprise, and the Welbeck Restaurant. This was distinct from the residents' dining room on the first floor, and served working women who were not residents. The YWCA had opened its first restaurant in 1884, nearby on Mortimer Street, and restaurants for working women flourished in this period, often near hostels and providing a safe and respectable place for women to stay nourished while working in the city. Ames House provided a model for later YWCA projects, with a diversity of accommodation and service facilities under one roof.

The Edwardian hostels featured either small bedrooms or cubicles, each with a single bed and limited furniture such as a washstand, wardrobe and wooden chair. Rooms or cubicles could be rented by the night but they were more normally rented by the week and on a long-term basis. The accommodation options suited different budgets: a cubicle at Brabazon House in 1915 cost 5s. 6d. per week, while single bedrooms cost between 7s. 6d. and 14s. a week; cubicles at Ada Lewis House were much less cost: between 3s. and 4s. per week. In line with the improving and protective spirit in which they were established, hostels were closely managed, usually with a matron, and sometimes with turnstiles for entry (as in the Rowton houses). Larger houses even had a nurse and servants. Requirements for entry were generally proof of employment but most hostels maintained a moral commitment to house women safely without income conditions.

Residents did, however, complain of regulations and the author of *The Bachelor Girl's Guide to Everything* (1917) set out the advantages of hostel living as lots of companionship, while the drawbacks were little privacy and 'irksome rules' about behaviour, curfews and guests (presumably men!).[19] Meals were shared communally in comfortable dining rooms which, in contrast to the necessarily spare cubicles and bedrooms, were the most architecturally ornamented rooms in the building, as seen at Brabazon House with its colonnaded alcove (**Fig. 7**). For an additional cost of around 10 shillings per week, residents were entitled to full board, thereby only having to seek out workday lunches on their own.

The 1911 census revealed that the average age of residents in Brabazon House was 30 and the most popular occupations were those of secretary, clerk, student and typist. The YWCA at Mortimer Street had a younger demographic with women averaging 25 years of age and mostly employed as dressmakers, milliners and teachers. A large percentage of the women were also servants in the house and, in the case of the YWCA, waitresses in the restaurant. The census roll provides a fascinating insight into the conversations the women

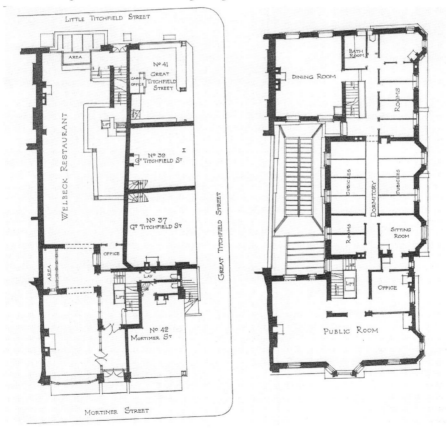

Fig. 8 Ames House, Mortimer Street, YWCA lodging house. 'Every little cubicle and bedroom has its own window and electric light – there is a wash-room, and a work-room containing provision for heating irons for the use of the boarders; the drawing room is kept for reading and music', noted an early twentieth-century resident, quoted in Kay Jenkinson's *Housing Women: A Celebration of YWCA Housing since 1855* (YWCA of Great Britain, 2000). Listed Grade II. [*The Builder,* 89 (1905) p. 396].

Fig. 9 Girls' Friendly Society, 29 Francis Street, Westminster. The prominent corner doorcase featured stone carving by H.C. Fehr and Ayling's trademark door plates with Art Nouveau flourishes. Listed Grade II. [Derek Kendall © English Heritage].

might have shared in the dining rooms of Brabazon House (where perhaps Violet Donaldson-Selby, a 26-year-old typist in the Colonial Office, and Emily Gribble, a 30-year-old stenographer for Remington typewriters slept on the same floor) and Ames House (where Daisy Frances Field, a 23-year-old assistant draper at Bourne and Hollingsworth and Evelina Maud Cox, a 25-year-old teacher at a LCC school might have eaten together). Despite the subtle distinctions between the accommodation and residents in different hostels, the buildings were united by a similarity of efficient and community-fostering plans, as well as handsome designs by architects and patrons who did their best to disguise the buildings' fairly institutional use.

In 1900 the GFS, founded in 1875 to offer support for young women who were new to urban life, had seven hostels with cubicles across west London. A decade later, this stalwart Victorian institution realised that it needed to keep up with the changing urban realm for young women, and planned a larger hostel near Victoria Station. It was also designed by Ayling – by then seemingly proficient with the building type which he had helped to develop – and it opened in 1914 at 29 Francis Street (**Fig. 9**). The bold Wrennaissance style hostel accommodated about 80 young women and featured well-dressed elevations with vibrant rubbed red brick and Portland stone quoins that nodded to the polychromy of nearby Westminster Cathedral. Inside, the upper-ground-floor rooms had simple fireplaces and the accommodation was in bedrooms rather than cubicles, indicating it was for middle-class 'respectable working women and girls' albeit those on a small budget. There was a stained glass window in one of the second floor communal rooms, which urged the young women to 'KEEP INNOCENCY', as displayed in a scroll beneath a dove. The hostel featured a separate exterior door for outside members to patronise it as a restaurant, as in the YWCA, and a waiting room where girls who came into town as new passengers on the early morning workmen's trains could wait in safety and comfort for their working day to begin.

In the suburbs, women's lodgings largely blossomed after the First World War but the Edwardian Waterlow Court, Baillie Scott's remarkable project for the Improved Industrial Dwellings Company, is worth mentioning here. Built in 1907-9, this sophisticated courtyard development was fully infused with the Arts and Crafts architectural spirit with attention to detail from door furniture and historicist staircases, through to overall planning of the open, arcaded cloister. The women residents were housed in three- to five-room flats, which was considerably more space and luxury than the inner-London hostels of the same date. Even the bicycles had more room and the purpose-built bicycle shed charmingly exhibited the architectural treatment of this other new building type used by the residents of Waterlow Court who exemplified the modern Edwardian way.

ADA LEWIS WOMEN'S LODGING HOUSE

The National Association of Women's Lodging Houses and its campaigners finally achieved the building they had sought for at least a decade in 1913 – the Ada Lewis Women's Lodging House (**Fig. 10**). Municipal funding for a women's lodging house had been long-sought, but the money ultimately

Fig. 10 Ada Lewis Women's Lodging House, exterior. Joseph & Smithem's design referred to its seventeenth-century sources through red-brick walls with stone dressings and tall round-arched windows under keystones. Listed Grade II. [Author].

Fig. 11 Ada Lewis Women's Lodging House, *Daily Mirror* photograph of sitting room *c*.1913. The portrait of the patron, Ada Lewis, was hung on the glazed tiled walls. This room has integral fireplaces which help create a grand and comfortable space amongst the other, practical common rooms.

came from the private source of Ada Lewis, a wealthy Jewish philanthropist who shared her peers' concerns about the lack of decent housing for single, low-waged working women.

On 28 January 1913, the Ada Lewis Women's Lodging House, a 'Hotel for Working Women and Girls' was opened by HRH Princess Louise.[20] This building marked a significant shift in the provision of housing for low-waged working women in London. It finally made available accommodation on the same relative scale as in the legendary Rowton Houses for men. This hostel, designed by the architects Joseph and Smithem and located near the Elephant and Castle, catered for 220, which made it the largest lodging house for women in London at that time. Ada Lewis House was special for offering modest yet architecturally-proud accommodation to twice the number of women at about half the price as was available previously. Its construction represented a dramatic response to a pressing need and it belongs to an important chapter in the provision of living space in the capital at a time of major social changes and opportunities for women.

The architects designed an imposing Baroque building of six storeys and a 'U'-plan. The seemingly generous upper-floor windows belied the paired tiny cubicles behind and the external effect was one of grandeur, noted in the pedimented main entrance reached by semi-circular steps. This historicist style conferred a sense of authority that fitted its semi-institutional use, yet the rich detailing produced a proud building to suit the women it housed. Joseph and Smithem employed the fireproof Mouchel-Hennebique ferro-concrete, then a relatively new material, which was visually apparent in the columns, beams and stairway partitions. To soften this robustness, the many communal rooms were lined with glazed tiles incorporating swags, pilasters, arched niches, and decorative tiled fireplaces (**Fig. 11**). Through the turnstile entrance was a stair with elaborate iron balustrade that continued the height of the building and lent it an air of ostentation.

Ada Lewis House provided a wide range of cost-saving and improving facilities including a sewing room, clothes-brushing room, foot baths, laundry and drying rooms that were celebrated for drying a resident's clothes within minutes of her coming in from the rain. The sleeping accommodation was on the first four floors, arranged efficiently and austerely along both sides of the U-plan corridor with bathrooms at the end of the wings (**Fig. 12**). When built, there were 214 single cubicles, twenty double bedrooms and six slightly larger 'special' rooms.

Within the first year, the trustees realised that the special bedrooms were

Fig. 12 Ada Lewis Lodging House, New Kent Road. Corridor with cubicles c.1913. The partitions in the cubicles were constructed with a gap at the bottom and a metal grille at the top to further air circulation through the densely populated accommodation wings. [London Metropolitan Archives, LMA/4318/B/03/006].

constantly let, but the cubicles less so. The very low-waged girls and women that the hostel had hoped to attract were not using Ada Lewis House. The trustees commented that the hostel was not being 'patronised by the poorest women so much as by those in rather more comfortable circumstances … teachers, typists, telephone clerks, and nurses there were plenty, but singularly few of the workers who chiefly need cheap, as well as respectable, sleeping accommodation'.[21] It was not long before the issue of gaps in the partitions was raised, and four months after opening the trustees commissioned Joseph and Smithem, to fill the lower opening. The poorest working women were soon designed out of the building.

The interior of Ada Lewis House was clearly modelled on the men's Rowton Houses which were also much evoked in the opening literature. Ada Lewis House was more inviting and 'feminine' in some of its decorative schemes, for example the mauve tiles with Art Nouveau flourishes, but the glazed tile dados, seemingly endless corridors of identical cubicles and even the bedspreads with circular logos were eerily similar. Earlier buildings had been hailed as the first 'women's Rowton', but Ada Lewis House was the first to carry it out.

A few months after Ada Lewis House opened, another hostel with aristocratic associations and royal connections – the Mary Curzon Home for Women – was introduced in Kings Cross. The hostel was built for the 'respectable poor' in memory of Lady Curzon of Kedleston, the American aristocrat and wife of Lord Curzon.[22] Queen Alexandra opened the building in November 1913 and the Curzon patronage was announced in the prominent frieze beneath the dormers (traces of 'women' is just legible beneath the black paint). This fairly institutional building at 170 Kings Cross Road accommodated 55 women in 40 cubicles: however, as at Ada Lewis House, a later second wave of residents demanded that the cubicles be enclosed for greater privacy.

During the First World War, the housing needs for women greatly increased as they moved to urban areas to engage with the war effort. The Association's report of 1915 described how 'the strain of the war has rendered (their hostels) abundantly useful.'[23] Although planned before the war, a home for 'educated women workers', Nutford House, opened in 1916, citing 'the increasing number of occupations now being thrown open to educated women such as schoolmistresses, students, secretaries, shorthand typists and manageresses of small businesses'.[24] The hostel on Brown Street in Lisson Grove was designed by Victor Wilkins who exhibited his design at the Royal Academy in 1915. It was an impressive building in a busy Wrennaissance style with deep dentilled cornice and stone quoins – the quality particularly noteworthy given the wartime conditions in which it opened. Private bedrooms accommodated around 100 women and one matron, but all other facilities were shared

Fig. 13 Furnival House, Cholmeley Avenue, Highgate. Listed Grade II. [Geoff Brandwood].

including a large social room with a beamed ceiling and fireplace, lounge, library and dining room that together took up most of the ground floor and basement. Another feature was the vast range of bicycle stores under the pavement – fourteen individual vaults, seven feet by ten feet wide, surely enough for each of the hundred residents to store a bicycle.

The following year a suburban development illustrated the continued foresight of the Prudential Assurance Company, which had been the first to employ ladies as clerks in 1871. On the leafy slopes of Highgate Hill in 1916, the company founded a hostel for the domestic workers at its Holborn Bars headquarters. Called Furnival House (**Fig. 13**), the Prudential motto and crest were featured in the lavishly plastered entrance hall of this Baroque-style hostel designed by Joseph Henry Pitt. Initially intended for the women who prepared the meals and stoked the fires at one of the country's foremost companies instead of the lady clerks who punched the cards, this grand building presented the residents with a bucolic alternative to the bustle of contemporary commercial life.

CONCLUSION

All of these women's lodgings essentially took the model of the middle class Victorian home and inflated it to cater to a larger community, but the hostels had formal architectural differences that identified them with different classes of working women. The late nineteenth-century chambers for middle class women had limited communal spaces, usually only shared dining rooms and bigger bedrooms arranged as bed–sitting rooms or even flats. These women gained a valuable sense of community from the limited shared facilities, but they maintained private respectability in their generous private quarters.

The working-class and lower-middle-class hostels for women that followed mostly housed women in cubicles, and the bedroom options were necessarily very small, which meant there were more shared common rooms for a variety of improving activities. Ada Lewis House had the greatest number of communal rooms – for sewing, reading, writing and sitting, as well as dining – and it was the first hostel on anything like the scale or plan of the working-class men's lodging houses, which had large amounts space given over to smoking and reading as well as dining. Regardless of the class of their residents, the ladies' chambers and the women's hostels generally shared several things: good architectural pedigree, and wealthy patrons that possessed strong business plans, a well-intentioned motive of protecting young women, but with a positive side effect of encouraging independence.

As Mary Higgs wrote in 1910, the women forced to the streets through lack of decent housing presented a dire scene: 'How far away from this the happy, pure home, an Englishwoman's heritage!' But the hostels that she and others promoted after the turn of the century were more than 'lighthouses' to prevent such wrecks of womanhood. Their tiny bedrooms and generous living rooms offered an empowering sanctuary of camaraderie in an exciting – but sometimes menacing – new modern world. The architects and patrons of these new buildings provided sound, attractive and comfortable lodgings that allowed a new generation of working women to satisfactorily answer Mary Higgs' question, 'where shall she live?'

Notes

1. Mary Higgs, *Glimpses into the Abyss,* London, 1906, pp. 194-5.
2. Mary Higgs and Edward E. Hayward, *Where Shall She Live? The Homelessness of the Woman Worker,* London, 1910, p. 180.
3. Sarah Kemp, Charlotte Mitchell & David Trotter, *Edwardian Fiction: An Oxford Companion,* Oxford, 1997, pp. xiii-xiv.
4. Duncan Crow, *The Edwardian Woman,* 1978, p. 142 footnote.
5. Higgs & Hayward, *Where Shall She Live?,* p. 3; Duncan Crow, *The Edwardian Woman,* 1978, p. 143.
6. Maude Stanley, *Clubs for Working Girls,* London, 1904, p. 208.
7. 'A Castle in the Air', *Work and Leisure: The Englishwoman's Advertiser, Reporter and Gazette,* 12:9, 1888, p. 235.
8. Ibid.
9. 'The Ladies' Dwellings Company, Limited', *Englishwoman's Review,* 15 March 1889, p. 141.

10. 'Sloane Gardens House', *Work and Leisure: The Englishwoman's Advertiser, Reporter & Gazette*, 14:11, 1889, p. 287.

11. Lynne Walker, 'The Entry of Women into the Architectural Profession in Britain', *Woman's Art Journal,* 7:1, 1986, pp. 13-18; Lynne Walker reports that the Chambers' drawings held in the RIBA Drawings Collection record York Street Chambers as their professional address.

12. Notes of Joint Sub-Committee on Lodging Houses for Women no. 2 in LCC Housing Department report (5 May 1901), LCC/MIN/7382.

13. LCC Housing of the Working Classes Committee Papers. LCC Public Health Department report (9 February 1910), LCC/MIN/7428.

14. Ella Hepworth Dixon, *The Story of a Modern Woman*, London, 1894, pp. 84-5.

15. Flora Klickmann, *The Ambitions of Jenny Ingram: A True Story of Modern London Life*, London, 1907, p. 285.

16. 'Brabazon-House (Limited)', *The Times*, 27 July 1903.

17. 'Obituary R. Stephen Ayling, FRIBA', *Journal of the Royal Institute of British Architects*, 39, 1932, pp. 859-60.

18. *Building News,* 89, 1905, p. 865.

19. Agnes M. Miall, *The Bachelor Girl's Guide to Everything or The Girl on Her Own*, London, 1916.

20. 'Homes for Working Women', *Morning Post*, 29 January 1913.

21. London Metropolitan Archives, LMA/4318/B/02/003, 'A Visit to the Ada Lewis House' by Cicely Ford, seemingly in the *Millgate Monthly* but undated journal extract tucked inside 'Scheme for the Administration and Management of the Ada Lewis Women's Lodging Houses'.

22. 'Queen Alexandra and a Women's Hostel', *The Times*, 24 November 1913, p. 5.

23. Mary Higgs & Edward E. Hayward, *The Housing of the Woman Worker*, London, 1915, p.11.

24. 'Educated Women Workers', *The Times,* 15 March 1913, p. 10.

6 Eclectic Visions and Elevated Ideals: Museums and Galleries

BARBARA LASIC

The nineteenth century was unquestionably the golden age of new museums and galleries and saw the emergence of an unprecedented number of such institutions across Europe and America. In Britain, this development was largely the result of a sustained effort, both governmental and private, aimed at educating the nation at large. However, in comparison to the continent, Britain's attempts to provide museums and galleries accessible to the general public were belated: while the Louvre opened its doors in 1793, it took Britain more than thirty years to establish its own national gallery, prompting a host of comments on the 'disgrace of England possessing no National Gallery for the reception of the choicest works of modern artists, as well as the finest of ancient masters, as in France'.[1] In Britain, the Museum Act of 1845 was fundamental in shaping the formation of public museums and galleries. It granted public funds to museums by allowing, for the first time, local authorities to use taxes to maintain libraries and museums, and signalled the beginning of the governmental support of the cultural field. Central to this impetus was the notion of the moralising influence of museums and galleries upon society, and the perceived benefits of bringing culture to the masses.

Victorian museums and galleries were often significant architectural monuments in their own right. Within their walls these newly founded sites represented a wide range of disciplines and deployed an extensive array of exhibits across both the social and the traditional sciences, ranging from the fine and decorative arts, to natural history, medicine and anatomy. Perhaps unsurprisingly, these edifices were characterised by an eclectic range of architectural styles. In fact, the well-known and amply studied 'battles of styles', so often discussed by architectural historians, were also being played out in the field of museum and gallery architecture. Greek revival or Queen Anne, Gothic versus Romanesque, the choice of style and architect, crystallised current concerns and expectations regarding the appropriate display of museum objects. Despite the 'genealogical' link between the older royal and aristocratic galleries and the new public museums (more of which later), the latter, because of their scale and purpose, required designs for which there were essentially no real precedents.

The nineteenth century, then, was a time when the notion of an architecture specific to museums and galleries came to the fore, although it remained a sub-theme of a broader discourse concerned with public architecture at large. More specifically, a body of literature emerged highlighting the importance of the practicality and suitability of museums and galleries over their grandeur and magnificence.[2] The notion of a blank canvas that would not overshadow the works on display was regularly discussed, as exemplified by the comments of the painter and arts administrator, Richard Redgrave (1804-88):

> it may be asked, what … is the cause that galleries for the reception of pictures have been so frequently failures as to the proper display of the works they contain? I believe it to be simply this. The architect is too often more intent upon displaying himself, and what he improperly considers his art, than the works for which the structure was intended … in a gallery for art, the art is the one thing to which all should be subservient: the pictures, in this case, are not meant to serve as subsidiary decorations to the architecture, but are themselves the jewels for which the building forms only a fitting and suitable casket.[3]

There were two particular concerns in relation to nineteenth-century museum and gallery architecture: the need to provide adequate lighting, and display space. Both led to the widespread use of top-lighting, which, among other things, diminished reflective glares on paintings and simultaneously maximised the wall space. The nineteenth century was also characterised by significant sanitary improvements, and the provision of adequate ventilation became a crucial feature of major new buildings. For instance, the 1861 Report of the Science and Art Department in relation to the building of the North and South Courts at the South Kensington Museum noted that 'the ventilation should be so perfect as not only to ensure equability of temperature, but also that the products of gas combustion, and the exhalations from large crowds of visitors should be thoroughly and speedily carried off, while at the same time the deteriorating effects of a London atmosphere should be as much as possible avoided.'[4]

The architecture of museums and galleries was much affected by technological improvements. New industrial processes of manufacture made most materials available in greater quantities and at cheaper prices, iron frames, for example, facilitating the development of taller buildings and allowing more open interior spaces which were ideal for display spaces. Yet no real architectural consensus was reached, prompting a journalist to write in the *The Architect* in 1892 that 'hitherto the nature of most English Museums has been

Fig. 1 Plan and elevation for the design for the capital and cornice of the Fitzwilliam Museum, Cambridge.

determined by chance or accident. From its title each of them was supposed to be dedicated to all the muses, but in reality they were left at the disposal of blind fortune'.[5]

The topic of museum and gallery architecture in nineteenth-century Britain is a vast and complex one and this paper can present only an overview beginning with a look at the styles that were deployed.

THE LURE OF THE CLASSICAL

Even a cursory study of museums built in the nineteenth century is enough to confirm the dominance of the classical vocabulary. William Wilkins' National Gallery (1832-8); Charles Cockerell's unapologetically Hellenistic Ashmolean (1841-5), considered as one of the last significant examples of the revival of Greek architecture; William Henry Playfair's National Gallery in Edinburgh (1859); and Cornelius Sherlock's Walker Art Gallery in Liverpool (1874-7), to name but a few, are all imposing neo-classical buildings. It was Robert Smirke's British Museum (1823-52) in particular which firmly established the 'classic museum type'.[6] Conceived as an immutable edifice indifferent to the disparate geographical and cultural artefacts displayed within its confines, its extensive Ionic facade is a constant reminder of the origins of the 'musea' as a Greek temple devoted to the muses. Its appearance was, however, not unanimously acclaimed and the architect James Fergusson scathingly remarked that 'nothing

[…] can well be more absurd than forty-four useless columns, following the sinuosities of a modern façade, and finishing round the corner [...] simply because the expense would not allow of its being carried further'.[7]

The Fitzwilliam Museum in Cambridge (1837-48) is another significant example of the nineteenth-century re-interpretation of classical architecture with rich architectural effects. Designed by George Basevi and finished by C.R. Cockerell after his death, it boasts an imposing Corinthian portico extended by short colonnades terminating in richly modelled pavilions. The museum's lavish façade marked a sharp contrast with its somewhat modest and understated side elevations. Inside, the galleries were articulated around a monumental staircase hall occupying a large part of the space (nearly a quarter of both floors) (**Fig. 1**).

The pre-eminence of the classical vocabulary for public buildings was, of course, not confined to Britain. By the first half of the nineteenth century, a lavish and monumental neoclassicism based on both Greek and Roman styles, had established itself on the Continent. Its suitability stemmed partly from its association with the classical roots of modern European culture, and also its exalted position in the hierarchy of styles.[8] It is easy to understand how it seemed to offer an apposite setting for canonical art works and material remains.

THE DULWICH PICTURE GALLERY

The Dulwich Picture Gallery is an admirable example of the marriage of classical architectural form and high culture. Opened in 1817, it is Britain's first purpose-built gallery and its erection marked a watershed in the history of museum architecture (**Fig. 2**). It was designed by Sir John Soane to house the collection formed by the art dealer and collector Noel Desenfans (1745-1807) and his business associate, Sir Francis Bourgeois, R.A. (1757-1811). Soane's friendship with Bourgeois lay behind his selection as the architect, and archival records reveal Bourgeois' wish to give the commission to his friend.[9] Soane's task consisted of rebuilding the west wing of Dulwich College to incorporate a gallery and almshouses, and also to provide a mausoleum for Bourgeois and the Desenfans family.

Surviving elevations, plans and perspective views trace the evolution of Soane's vision, a vision which was significantly altered and hindered by lack of funds.[10] The final structure boasted five galleries *en enfilade*, framed by two wings of lower building, with the mausoleum in the centre on the west façade, flanked left and right by almshouses.[11]

The architecture of the Dulwich Picture Gallery and the arrangement of rooms were in many respects rooted in the tradition of long picture galleries in major country houses. The proportions of the rooms were not dissimilar to those at Castle Howard and were consistent with Palladian principles. The succession of simple arches linking the rooms is also reminiscent of George Dance's Shakespeare Gallery in London, home of the short-lived British Institution.[12] The top-lit rectangular room remained the standard design for picture galleries in the nineteenth century and allowed the comfortable circulation of people. It was derived from Renaissance prototypes and had been widely employed in British private galleries from the eighteenth century onwards.[13] The enfilade of rooms, often alternating rectangular and square rooms, developed from this pattern and was eagerly embraced by nineteenth-century continental museums, particularly German ones, such as the Alte Pinakothek in Munich. Another type of arrangement deriving from the plan mentioned above consisted of a series of parallel rooms arranged around a central core, or parallel enfilades of rooms linked by transverse galleries, as exemplified by the Lady Lever Gallery in Port Sunlight.[14]

The Dulwich Picture Gallery is an important prototype for later institutions. It broke with the established tradition of displaying paintings on the first floor and displayed them instead on the ground floor. Like Soane's earlier designs for William Beckford's picture gallery at Fonthill Splendens, the gallery at Dulwich ingeniously incorporated the use of top lighting to maximise the availability of wall space and provide suitable light (**Fig. 3**).[15] Thermal zones also delineated the various sections of the building: the gallery was heated centrally with steam, the almshouses had fireplaces, whilst the mausoleum remained unheated.[16]

Yet the gallery was also in some respects very much unlike any other early nineteenth-century museum inasmuch as it combined the dual function of museum and mausoleum.[17] Soane welcomed its inclusion in the commission.[18] He used the understated Greek Doric order and avoided Christian symbolism. The skylight was glazed with yellow glass to create a 'dull, religious light' that would evoke 'the funereal grandeur' and the economy of decoration gracefully conveys 'the recollections of past times'.[19]

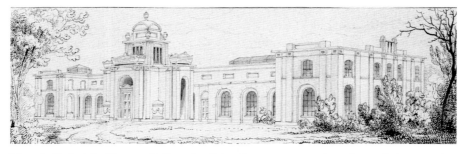

Fig. 2 Dulwich Picture Gallery by John Soane: perspective view of the exterior showing the west and south façade as built.

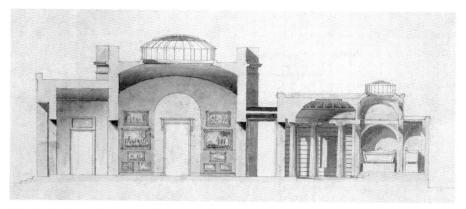

Fig. 3 Dulwich Picture Gallery: lateral section through the domed central bay of the picture gallery and the mausoleum in a preliminary version.

Although one might easily see the correlation between, say, the priceless Old Masters exhibited in the country's national galleries, and the elevated architectural vocabulary of their structures, the story is more complex. Even more modest municipal museums, far removed from the high culture of the Victorian art world, succumbed to the lure of the classical. For example, when faced with their relocation, the collections of the Manchester City Art Gallery happily moved in 1882 to Charles Barry's neo-Grecian Royal Manchester Institution.[20] The classical idiom crystallised the enlightenment construct of the organisation of things and knowledge, and might have therefore been perceived as being fit to house carefully selected and meticulously ordered exhibits. In addition, the use of the classical vocabulary emphasised the analogy between the technological and social advancements of the nineteenth century and the achievements of the great civilisations of the past.

THE GOTHIC REVIVAL AND MUSEUM ARCHITECTURE

Given the impact of the Gothic Revival on nineteenth-century British architecture, it is surprising that so few museums and galleries were erected in this style. In fact, only two out of ten designs submitted as part of the competition to design the new National Gallery in 1866 were in the Gothic idiom, namely those of Somers Clarke and G. E. Street. This prompted the latter's son to note that 'it seemed to be assumed either that Gothic was not suitable for the particular purpose, or that the surrounding in Trafalgar Square made the adoption of a style so different unadvisable'.[21]

There were, however, a few notable exceptions, and the University Museum at Oxford, opened in 1860, was one of them. Out of twelve competition designs, the Gothic Revival drawings of the Irish architect Benjamin Woodward of Deane and Woodward were selected for the new building which was intended to house the university's natural history collections, and also professors' offices, a laboratory, a library and a lecture room for the benefits of both students and the academic faculty.[22] The building committee supervising the new building

Fig. 4 View of the central court of the Oxford University Museum.

Fig. 5 Natural History Museum by Alfred Waterhouse, 1876.

felt that the interplay between new sciences and 'old' architecture was highly suitable. Not only did the contents of the museum echo the 'natural forms' present in the architecture of the building, but the latter also evoked the city's past.[23] The entrance block with its central tower is strongly reminiscent of Flemish town halls. Its glass and iron roof was specifically devised to maximise the flow of natural light. It creates a striking contrast with the polychrome stonework and the delicate ironwork of the virtuoso craftsman Francis Skidmore. The central court is framed by the statues of eminent men, and surrounded by columns decorated with carvings representing the different botanical orders (**Fig. 4**). Despite the use of iron, the design of the museum, its use of polychromy and the treatment of the carvings and ornament which demonstrated a close study of nature, were informed by Ruskinian principles.[24] The museum was intrinsically didactic and each column was labelled to teach visitors to recognise the different types of stones used. The function of the building was therefore dual: it was both an architectural frame and an exhibit in its own right.

AN ECLECTIC VISION: ALBERTOPOLIS

Museum architecture in the nineteenth century went beyond the dichotomy of classical versus Gothic and encompassed a more eclectic interpretation and free utilisation of past styles, as exemplified by the Natural History Museum (**Fig. 5**) and the South Kensington Museum, renamed Victoria & Albert Museum in 1899 (**Fig. 6**).

The two museums were built as part of a complex cultural and urban

Fig. 6 The Entrance to the South Kensington Museum, 1869.

quarter on the 87 acres purchased by the Commissioners of the 1851 Great Exhibition, partly with the surplus of the exhibition and partly with funds granted by Parliament.[25] The scheme, also known as Albertopolis due to Prince Albert's seminal involvement, was the most ambitious of its kind at the time in Britain. It was intended as a centre for provision of culture and knowledge and arguably marked the apogee of the Governmental monumental efforts to democratise culture and the arts.

Both the concept of Albertopolis and the buildings that constituted it were revolutionary in their own right. The South Kensington Museum was indeed the first museum of applied arts in Britain and one of the first monumental museum buildings to eschew the neoclassical style. The unpopular 'Brompton Boilers', a prefabricated iron structure, were soon complemented and eventually replaced by a series of permanent buildings designed by Francis Fowke, and Henry Scott after the former's death. This ambitious plan culminated with the building of the North and South Courts, and a block incorporating a lecture theatre which served as the museum façade until the erection of the Aston Webb building in 1909 (**Fig. 7**).

The architecture and decoration of the V&A synthesized a wide range of influences. Faced with red brick, terracotta and mosaics, the overall style of the Quadrangle erected as part of Fowke's and Scott's plans, was unequivocally

Italianate. Godfrey Sykes's terracotta columns in the Science Schools recall those of the loggia of the Cologne rathaus, described by Henry Cole in his diary as 'a picturesque mixture of Italian & cinquecento work' (**Fig. 8**).[26]

The decoration of the museum was in the hands of a team of in-house designers, supported by students of the School of Design which was attached to the Museum. They employed a rich palette of techniques. For instance, the South Court skilfully juxtaposed large-scale mosaic portraits of famous artists with frescoes painted by Lord Leighton representing the Industrial Arts as Applied to War and Peace.[27] Some of the greatest artists of the day were solicited to contribute to the decorative scheme: the Green Dining Room was decorated by William Morris' firm, Morris, Marshall, Faulkner & Co, and with stained glass windows designed by Edward Burne-Jones. The west staircase was another *tour de force,* albeit a controversial one: designed by F.W. Moody, it

Fig. 7 Victoria and Albert Museum, the Aston Webb façade.

was entirely encased in Della Robbia ware and mosaics. Minton's new process of vitrified ceramic painting was employed on the ceiling, domes, wall panels and spandrels.[28]

The lavish decorative schemes devised at South Kensington Museum made it an aesthetic exemplar in its own right which exerted an unparalleled influence on the architecture of decorative arts museums in Europe, the Museum für Kunst und Industrie in Vienna in particular (**Fig. 9**), and America such as the Cincinnatti Art Museum or the Museum of Fine Arts in Boston.

Across the road, a no less imposing and palatial building was being erected. The Natural History Museum, designed by Alfred Waterhouse, was in fact the first completed building on the South Kensington site.[29] The choice of an hybrid Romanesque style was informed by contemporary practice as well as a complex interplay of social, aesthetic and political considerations. Its constructional polychromy was an architectural triumph. The extensive use of terracotta panels on its interiors and exteriors, a bold step on such a large building, was intended to resist the sooty climate of Victorian London.[30] Terracotta was indeed not just a relatively cheap material, but it was also greatly valued for its perceived durability. Like the Oxford University Museum, the structure of the Natural History Museum is reminiscent of medieval town halls, but the museum portal also evokes the grand entrances of Romanesque churches.[31] Waterhouse was determined to keep an architectural simplicity that would best showcase 'the evolution of primitive forms of life into the most

Fig. 8 The South Kensington Museum, arcade on the first floor of the Science Schools.

Fig. 9 Exterior of the Austrian Museum of Art and Industry, Vienna.

sophisticated'.[32] He was also concerned that the museum structure provided enough natural light as galleries would not include gas lights. The panels and bricks feature many relief sculptures of flora and fauna, with living and extinct species featured within the west and east wings respectively. These were designed by Hungerford Pollen and strongly recall the decorative treatment of the Oxford University Museum.[33] Here we see that the educational purpose of the museum was fully reflected by its architecture. The relationship between the museum's mission, contents and physical structure was dynamic and fluid, and sought to unify the museum experience by bringing together what was viewed and where it was viewed.

Albertopolis was unequivocally didactic and its creation prepared the ground for a large number of smaller institutions with educational aims in mind. Indeed, as the century drew to a close, a new type of public gallery emerged, one principally aimed at working class audiences and removed from the scholarly grandeur or imposing classical magnificence of the buildings just discussed.

PHILANTHROPIC GALLERIES AND HOUSE MUSEUMS

The South London Gallery is a good example of such an institution, being almost exclusively the product of a philanthropic impulse to be found in public galleries in some of the poorest urban areas. The South London Gallery was indeed the brainchild of the philanthropist and local tradesman William Rossiter who had contributed to the establishment of Working Men's College in Great Ormond Street. Founded in 1868 as the South London Working Men's College, its primary mission was to provide culture to the poorer segments of society. It underwent several incarnations and bore several names before being permanently established at its current location in Camberwell.[34]

It opened on Peckham Road in May 1891, and in discussing its opening, a journalist noted that 'the success of the Gallery demonstrated its necessity'.[35] Tantalisingly, little is known of its early structure. A lecture room designed by Sir Ernest George of George & Peto was added in 1893 to the existing top-lit gallery and small 'museum room'. An illustration of the lecture room published in the *Building News* in 1893 shows that it was in the baronial style with a queen post roof, and that the motto 'work in faith, faith in work' was inscribed above the minstrel's gallery.[36] The gallery boasted an elegant inlaid parquet floor designed by Walter Crane (**Fig. 10**) with a central panel inscribed 'The Source of Art is in the Life of a People'. The walls of the main rooms were divided into two horizontal sections, the lower one being devoted to the display of paintings. According to the *Building News*, the decorative scheme was influenced by the painters Edward Burne-Jones and Wyke Bayliss, and included wallpaper by Woollams & Co. and Jeffreys & Co.

The most significant changes to the gallery occurred under the auspices

Fig. 10 Walter Crane's design for the inlaid wood floor for the South London Fine Art Gallery.

122

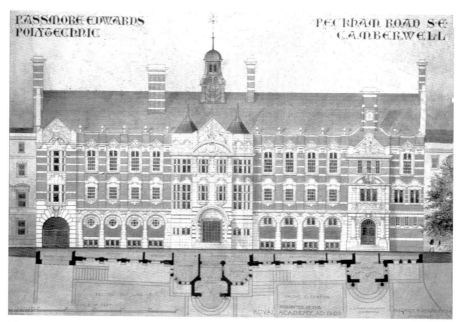

PASSMORE EDWARDS POLYTECHNIC

PECKHAM ROAD S·E· CAMBERWELL

Fig. 11 The South London Gallery. [Southwark Art Collection: South London Gallery Permanent Collection].

of the architect Maurice Bingham Adams who, in 1896, was commissioned to extend the current building to reflect its informal amalgamation with a technical institute (later to become the Camberwell School of Art) founded in memory of Lord Leighton. Adams designed the building for the new institute, as well as the front part of the galleries to which he added an office for the curator, a cloakroom and an entrance vestibule. Commenting on the new plans, Edward Foskett, the Chief Librarian, remarked that 'while meeting the requirements of an Art School, [they] also bring order out of the chaotic condition of the existing building'.[37] Adams' close links with the newspaper magnate and philanthropist John Passmore Edwards, who sponsored the Institute, no doubt secured him the commission.[38] Adams had previously worked with Norman Shaw and was a faithful exponent of the Queen Anne style which he employed for the South London Gallery.

Comparing the plans published in the *Building News* in 1896 with the completed building reveals that Adams did not stick to his original ideas. The inscription in the cartouche over the door in the early scheme emphasised the importance of the gallery, whereas the built site gave pre-eminence to the Technical Institute. The entrance of the institute was proudly framed by atlantes supporting a protruding arch, above which was 'an assertively decorative study of the use of curved windows in an adapted Tudor manner'.[39] On the other hand, the gallery was relegated to one side, two simple pilasters marking its entry (**Fig. 11**).

Another type of museum emerged in the nineteenth century: the 'house museum' intended to display the collections of their owners. Examples are numerous and cannot be grouped into one single architectural category. While John Soane's Museum remains a perfect and somehow restrained exemplar of classical splendour, Richard Wallace's house in Manchester Square, with its juxtaposition of original eighteenth-century French architectural fixtures and nineteenth-century replicas, crystallises the late Victorian re-interpretation of eighteenth-century century French aristocratic taste.

It is however, not in cosmopolitan London but in rural County Durham that one of the most extraordinary incarnations of the nineteenth-century taste for the French *Ancien Régime* can be found. On 27 November 1869, Josephine Benoite, countess of Montalbo, wife of John Bowes, laid the foundation stone of the Bowes Museum, the crowning achievement of their collecting activities and philanthropic aspirations. Envisaged as a northern counterpart to the South Kensington Museum, the Bowes Museum was eminently didactic and its purpose was the edification of the public. It contained the lavish collection of fine and decorative arts avidly assembled by the couple over a period of twelve years.[40] The building was unapologetically French (**Fig. 12**): it was designed by the Parisian architect Jules Pellechet (1829-1903) and executed by the Newcastle architect John Edward Watson (d.1885). This style, thought to epitomise elegance and refinement, had been eagerly adopted by British

Fig. 12 The Bowes Museum, Barnard Castle, Co. Durham, by the French architect Jules Pellechet, 1869-92. [Bowes Museum].

plutocrats for their residences, as exemplified by Ferdinand de Rothschild's Waddesdon Manor in Buckinghamshire (1874-89). Although the style had also been employed for public buildings and grand hotels, it had remained so far unused for museum and galleries in Britain.[41]

It seems that the Bowes were directly inspired by French buildings. A photograph of the destroyed Palais des Tuileries was used as a model for the arch at the entrance to the building.[42] A letter from the ceramicist Emile Gallé to Josephine brings the French connection to the fore: 'avez-vous donc voulu reconstruire nos pauvres Tuileries en Angleterre? C'est tout à fait le pavillon de Marsan. Quelle habitation princière et royale pour nos humbles faiences', adding that raising the roofs would enhance the visual impact of the bulding: 'les toits, surtout ceux des pavillons extrêmes, gagneront à être rehaussés [...] cette modification ajoutera plus encore au grandiose de l'ensemble'.[43] Detailed measurements and illustrations of Brunet-Debaine's town hall in Le Havre, famously nicknamed the 'petit Louvre', were also requested by John Bowes.[44]

Although the foundation stone was laid in 1869, a series of financial setbacks delayed the opening of the museum to the public until 1892. The rooms on the first floor were used for the display of the different branches of art manufacture, and the top-lit galleries on the second floor were, unsurprisingly, devoted to the display of paintings. In addition to the galleries, the building also included accommodation for the curator. Its palatial size and neo-renaissance style cut a striking figure both in the landscape of County Durham, and that of nineteenth-century museums. Commenting on it, Pevsner noted that its scale was 'just as gloriously inappropriate for the town to which it belongs [...] as in style'.[45]

By the end of the century, the extensive and eclectic use of historical styles elicited strong reactions among a number of architects, and prompted them to break with the past and seek a new original 'free style'.[46] These practitioners were more concerned with the honest use of building materials and the edifices they designed were characterised by a greater degree of simplicity and practicality. Such buildings can be loosely qualified as 'functionalist' inasmuch as their internal organisations informed and shaped what they looked like from the outside.

ARTS AND CRAFTS MUSEUMS AND GALLERIES

The Horniman Museum in Forest Hill, South London, which opened in 1901, is one of the most significant exemplars of Arts and Crafts architecture in Britain (**Fig. 13**). It was designed by the architect Charles Harrison Townsend (1851-1925) and described in *The Studio* as 'worthy of attention' and as a 'new series of frank and fearless thought expressed and coordinated into stone'.[47] The Horniman Museum has often been regarded as Townsend's greatest

Fig. 13 The Horniman Museum, London, by Charles Harrison Townsend, 1897-1901. [Horniman Museum].

achievement and 'the most remarkable example of a reckless repudiation of tradition among English architects at the time'.[48] Townsend was indeed a leading architect of the Arts and Crafts movement who later also designed the Whitechapel Art Gallery.[49] A member of the Art Workers' Guild, he was familiar with current debates on the perceived superiority of medieval craftsmanship and the perceived deleterious effects of mechanisation upon society. However, Townsend's own views were somehow tempered by a marked adherence to functionalist principles. In a lecture at the Architectural Association in 1902, he strongly rejected the copying of past styles and emphasised the importance of devising buildings based on needs.[50]

The Horniman Museum was founded by the philanthropist tea merchant

126

Frederick John Horniman to house his anthropological collections. His mission had been to bring the world to London, and his didactic project had effectively started in the early 1890s with the opening of his collection to the public within the confines of his own home. Eventually, the growth of the collections and the ever-increasing stream of visitors prompted Horniman to commission a purpose-built structure.

The construction of the museum was somewhat complicated by the fact that it was located on a long and narrow site on a steep slope. It was arranged around two large top-lit halls of equal size. The main entrance gave access to the south hall through an oval vestibule. A twelve-foot-high gallery ran around both halls. A corridor extended along the entire length of the building and communicated with each hall. Townsend's building also included a small exhibition room, a library, as well as store-rooms, a photographic darkroom and apartments for the caretaker and the resident curator. The museum was heated and electric lighting was installed throughout. The fireproof ceiling and floors were made of iron and concrete, and the floors were covered with wood blocks.

The imposing frontage and clock tower were built with Doulting stone whilst red brick was used for the remainder of the building. The tower, which contained an apartment over the entrance hall, begins with a square base and gradually adopts a circular shape. The lower frieze of leafy trees, a recurrent motif in Townsend's work, and the capitals of the façade borrow from the established vocabulary of Arts and Crafts ornament. A large decorative mosaic panel after designs by Robert Anning Bell (1863-1933) adorns the façade. An allegory of the course of human life, it shows the figure of Humanity being led out of the House of Circumstance by the allegorical figures of Poetry, Art, Music (**Fig. 14**). Also a member of the Arts Workers' Guild, Anning Bell was a seminal figure in the movement to revive the use of mosaics in architecture.[51] Below it is a bronze memorial tablet by F. W. Pomeroy, bearing the dedication

Fig. 14 Design by R. Anning Bell for the mosaic of the Horniman Museum, 1898.

of the museum and its collections to 'the public for ever … for their instruction and enjoyment'.

The Horniman Museum can be read as a synthesis of Townsend's views. The simplicity of its long brick flank walls and iron structural frame crystallise the architect's functional concerns to create a site intended for extensive public use. Yet the decorative treatment of façade and the inclusion of the mosaic frieze also reflects Townsend's adherence to the Arts and Crafts principles of favouring traditional craftsmanship and manual labour: the 117,000 pieces were hand-set on the wall over a period of 210 days.[52] The interplay between the nature of the collections exhibited at the Horniman Museum, and the principles that shaped the creation of the building is significant, the organic forms of its decorative treatment engaging in a silent dialogue with the exhibits.

The museums and galleries built in nineteenth-century Britain had a significant impact on the nation's culture and urban life. These ambitious schemes are a testament of the governmental and philanthropic impetus to bring art, science and, more generally, culture to the people. Temples of knowledge, these edifices testify to the resilience of their founders, architects and builders, and their skill at reconciling the demands of an ever increasing public, with the display requirements of their collections.

ACKNOWLEDGEMENTS

I wish to thank Christopher Marsden for his helpful comments, and Hayley Hegan from the Horniman Museum, Christopher Jordan from the South London Gallery, and Judith Phillips from the Bowes Museum, for kindly granting me access to their archives.

Except where stated all images are reproduced by kind permission of V&A Images/Victoria and Albert Museum.

Notes

1. *The Times*, 12 July 1831, p. 4.
2. Alistair Service, *Edwardian Architecture,* London, 1977, pp. 38–59, 102–17. Christopher Whitehead, 'Henry Cole's European Travels and the Building of the South Kensington Museum in the 1850s', *Architectural History*, 48, 2005, p. 194.
3. Cited in: Christopher Whitehead, *The Public Art Museum in Nineteenth-Century Britain,* Aldershot, 2005, p. 15.
4. John Physik, *The Victoria and Albert Museum. The History of its Building*, London, 1982, p. 48.
5. *The Architect*, 1 January 1892, p. 3.
6. Charles Saumarez Smith, 'Architecture and the Museum. The Seventh Reyner Banham Memorial Lecture', *Journal of Design History*, 8:4, 1995, p. 243.
7. James Fergusson, *History of Modern Styles of Architecture,* London, 1862, pp. 304–5.

8. Smith, *Architecture and the Museum*, p. 244

9. Giles Waterfield, *Soane and After. The Architecture of Dulwich Picture Gallery*, London, 1987, p. 8.

10. Francesco Nevola, *Soane's Favourite Subject: the Story of the Dulwich Picture Gallery*, London, 2000.

11. Bridget Cherry & Nikolaus Pevsner, *The Buildings of England. South London* Harmondswoth, 1984, p. 622

12. Waterfield, *Soane and After.* pp. 10-11.

13. Giles Waterfield, *Palaces of Art. Art Galleries in Britain 1790-1990*, London, 1991, p. 25.

14. Nikolaus Pevsner, *A History of Building Types,* London, 1976, pp. 127–30; Waterfield, *Palaces of Art,* p. 25.

15. Ibid.;. Waterfield, *Soane and After*, pp. 10-11. The mausoleum was also top-lit.

16. Todd Willmert, 'Heating Methods and their Impact on Soane's Work: Lincoln's Inn Fields and Dulwich Picture Gallery', *Journal of the Society of Architectural Historians*, 52:1, 1993, p. 52.

17. This inclusion resulted from the fact that Bourgeois could not secure the freehold of his house on Charlotte Street where a mausoleum also designed by Soane had originally been built.

18. Mausoleums were considered ideal structures by neoclassical architects. Howard Colvin, *Architecture and the After-Life*, New Haven & London, 1991, pp. 358-60. In fact, Soane had already designed a mausoleum in 1807 behind the house occupied by Bourgeois and the Desenfans, in what is now known as Hallam Street. The failure to secure the freehold prompted Bourgeois to commission one at Dulwich. See Pierre de la Ruffinière du Prey, *Sir John Soane. Catalogue of Architectural Drawings in the Victoria and Albert Museum*, London, 1985, pp. 80, 86-7.

19. John Soane, *Designs for Public and Private Buildings,* London, n.d., p. 48. Willmert, 'Heating Methods and their Impact on Soane's Work', p. 57

20. 'Manchester United', *The Burlington Magazine*, 144, 2002, p. 723

21. Arthur Edmund Street, *Memoir of George Edmund Street RA by his son Arthur Edmund Street*, London, 1888, p. 51.

22. Carla Yanni, *Nature's Museums: Victorian Science and the Architecture of Display*, London, 1999, p. 64. Sadly the competition drawings do not survive.

23. Ibid., pp. 72-5.

24. Ruskin's agency on the choice of the architect has been well documented: Yanni, *Nature's Museums*, p. 74.

25. Anthony Burton, *Vision and Accident. The Story of the Victoria and Albert Museum.* London, 1999.

26. Christopher Whitehead, 'Henry Cole's European Travels and the Building of the South Kensington Museum in the 1850s', *Architectural History*, 48, 2005, p. 217

27. The use of elaborate painted decorative schemes was not limited to the South Kensington Museum: the so-called Musée Charles X at the Louvre boasted elaborate painted ceilings, and the Alte Pinakothek in Munich was decorated by frescoes depicting the history of medieval and Renaissance European art. Physik, *The Victoria and Albert Museum*, p. 57.

28. Ibid., p. 126

29. Colin Cunningham & Prudence Waterhouse, *Alfred Waterhouse: 1830-1905. Biography of a Practice*, Oxford, 1992, p. 72.

30. They were manufactured by the Tamworth-based company of Gibbs & Canning Ltd, who also supplied tiles for the Albert Hall.

31. J.B. Bullen, 'Alfred Waterhouse's Romanesque 'Temple of Nature': the Natural History Museum. London', *Architectural History*, 49 2006, p. 269.

32. Ibid., p. 268.

33. Ibid., p. 279.

34. The South London Working Men's College opened on Blackfriars Road in 1868. It later moved to Kennington Lane in 1878. The first free library opened there the same year, and in 1879 Rossiter organised its first exhibition of privately owned works of art. Bolstered by its success, further exhibitions followed and eventually, the name of the institution was changed to Free Library & Art Gallery. It was temporarily housed in Battersea and then Camberwell Road before moving to its current site. For the full story of the foundation of the gallery, see Giles Waterfield (ed.), *Art for the People. Culture in the Slums of Late Victorian Britain,* London, 1994.

35. *The Times*, 11 November 1891, p. 5

36. *Building News,* 6 October 1893, p. 437. See also Waterfield (ed), *Art for the People*, p. 58.

37. South London Gallery Archive, Camberwell Commissioners of Free Public Libraries and Museums, Minute Book 2, 2/1896-5/1896, 11 March 1896.

38. Adams designed several libraries funded by Passmore Edwards and also worked for the *Building News* which was owned by Passmore Edwards. Waterfield (ed.), *Art for the People*, p. 60.

39. Ibid., p. 61.

40. Sarah Kane, 'Turning Bibelots into Museum Pieces: Josephine Coffin-Chevallier and the Creation of the Bowes Museum, Barnard Castle', *Journal of Design History,* 9:1, 1996, pp. 1-21.

41. J. Mordaunt Crook, *The Rise of the Nouveaux Riches. Style and Status in Victorian and Edwardian Architecture,* London, 1999, pp. 57-66.

42. Charles E. Hardy, *John Bowes and the Bowes Museum*, Newcastle upon Tyne, 1970, p. 161

43. Bowes Museum Archive, Gallé 3, letter dated 18 September 1871

44. Hardy, *John Bowes*, p. 161

45. Nikolaus Pevsner, *The Buildings of England. County Durham* (London, 1953), p. 47.

46. Service, *Edwardian Architecture, see* chapter 'The Free Style and Large Buildings', pp. 38-58. But the story is complex and exponents of the 'free style' also on occasion embraced historical idioms.

47. Alistair Service 'Arts and Crafts Extremis. Charles Harrison Townsend (1851-1925), *Architectural Association Quarterly,* 6:2, 1974, pp. 5-12. *The Studio*, 24, 1902, pp. 196-202.

48. Nikolaus Pevsner, *Pioneers of Modern Design from William Morris to Walter Gropius,* London, 1960, p. 165.

49. Townsend's other large commissions included the Bishopsgate Institute in London.

50. *The Builder*, 82, 1902, pp. 133–6. *Architectural Association Notes*, 17, 1902, pp. 33–9, 44.

51. Anning Bell later worked on the decoration of the Lady Chapel at Westminster Cathedral. Peyton Skipwith. 'Bell, Robert Anning' in *Grove Art Online. Oxford Art Online*, http://www.oxfordartonline.com/subscriber/article/grove/art/T007582 (accessed 6 March 2010).

52. Horniman Museum Archive, London. Conservation Plan by Allies & Morrison Architects, May 1998, p. 17.

7 From Caught to Court: Police Stations and Magistrates' Courts in London

SUSIE BARSON

M any Londoners will be familiar with the appearance of Victorian and Edwardian police stations and court buildings along London's main thoroughfares. What they may have noticed is the imposing demeanour of the exteriors – often characterised by a severe classical architectural style and a strong townscape presence, frequently located near other civic buildings. They may have even observed the family resemblance between some of the turn-of-the-century buildings designed by John Dixon Butler – perhaps the most accomplished and skilled designer of police stations and magistrates' courts – with fine Edwardian Baroque ensembles in Old Street, King's Cross Road, Tooley Street and Rochester Row. Some key questions emerge. Why do they look the way they do? How and why did the building type emerge? Who was responsible for the design? How did they function? What factors influenced their design? This chapter attempts, through a brief chronological account, to answer such questions.[1]

EARLY POLICING IN LONDON

The power to arrest and imprison evildoers was held, from the fourteenth century, by the Justices of Peace, men learned in the law, 'for the keeping of the peace in every shire of England.'[2] As it would have been impractical for the JPs to have arrested suspected criminals personally, a system of constables was introduced, willing volunteers whose duties were to carry out the instructions of the JPs, and to serve warrants and keep watch on their districts. These volunteers often consisted of the old, illiterate or infirm men: the 'Charlies', watchmen appointed in the City of London in the reign of Charles II, and notoriously ineffective. In 1673 an Act was passed authorising JPs to appoint petty constables, thereby statutorily authorising a custom that had long been in practice. Special constables could be sworn in for emergencies.

Parish watch houses had been erected from the late seventeenth and early eighteenth centuries by churchwardens who also had responsibility for their repair and maintenance. This duty was transferred to the parish beadles and constables in the 1730s. In 1736 an Act was passed to make the Westminster watch more effective and empowered the vestry to appoint as many watchmen as seemed necessary twice yearly.

In the eighteenth century there was an increase in the effectiveness of preventing crime and punishing offenders. In the mid-1730s, a London JP called Thomas De Veil set up a Justices' office at 4 Bow Street, adjacent to Covent Garden market. Although credited with taking this important step, De Veil did not command the respect of his contemporaries: Hogarth's depiction of a drunken De Veil in 1740 having to be escorted home, while scenes of crime are going on all around him, shows how little regard he had for the magistrate.

It was to this Bow Street office that Henry Fielding, the novelist and magistrate, moved in 1748, and set up a special band of constables a year later called the Bow Street Runners. This was London's first professional police force, just eight constables paid for by central government, and was an important move towards increasing the status of the police, and state intervention in street life. When Fielding died in 1754, management of the Bow Street office was taken over by his brother John, and under him the Bow Street Runners became a full-time paid force. A foot-patrol supervised the central area, and the horse patrol protected the main highways out of London.

Clearly this small force could not keep up with increasing crime in late eighteenth-century London. Following the Gordon Riots in June 1780, the anti-Catholic uprising that saw attacks on Newgate Prison and the Houses of Parliament, and which the military were brought in to quell, there was a realisation that the powers of the law had to be strengthened. The Middlesex Justices Act of 1792 provided for six public offices in addition to Bow Street, each with three paid JPs who were to employ sufficient constables for 'the more effectual prevention of felonies'.[3] Six was the average number of constables attached to these offices located at Hatton Garden, Worship Street in Whitechapel, Shadwell, Southwark, Queen Square, and Great Marlborough Street. These offices were a response to the need for the police officers not only to do away with the encouragement of crime afforded by the conduct of old magistrates as depicted by Hogarth, but also to 'clear the metropolis of pickpockets and various depredators who have for a long time disgraced the London magistracy'.[4]

By 1800 there were two types of police buildings in London: the administrative offices, with an adapted court room at the rear for the magistrates, most of which were formed in existing buildings, and watch houses and lock-ups for imprisoning criminals. Bow Street's courtroom, a tall narrow room with a gallery on one side and a raised seat at one end for the magistrate with the accused facing him, was enlarged and adapted until replaced by the purpose-built court of 1880. The building of watch houses continued into the nineteenth century, until they were eventually taken over by the new official police force established by Sir Robert Peel's Metropolitan Police Act of 1829 (**Fig. 1**). Another common practice was to form offices and cells within existing houses, as at Paradise Street, Rotherhithe (**Fig. 2**), built by William Gaitskell for his own use in 1814 and converted for police use in 1836.

PEEL AND THE METROPOLITAN POLICE ACT, 1829.

When Robert Peel joined Lord Liverpool's ministry as Home Secretary in 1821 he had already instituted the Irish Constabulary, nick-named 'Peelers'. He undertook criminal law reform and in February 1828 he set up a committee on the police system, which recommended that a Police Office be established for the entire Metropolis, under the direct control of the Home Secretary. This led to the Metropolitan Police Bill of April 1829, which received Royal Assent on 19 June. The Act had two aims: it stated that 'the primary object of an efficient police is the prevention of crime'; the next, 'that of detection and punishment of offenders if the crime is committed'.[5] The objective was to move away from the fragmented, amateur and *ad hoc* methods of criminal capture and trial towards an integrated system within the judicial process.

Peel failed to bring the City of London within the provisions of the Act, and also the River Police (set up in 1795 to combat smuggling) as well as

Fig. 1 Watch house at Wood Close, Bethnal Green, built in 1826 by the local churchwardens. Watch houses were often located close to the churchyards to deter grave robbers who supplied hospital medical schools with bodies. [London Metropolitan Archives].

Fig. 2 Paradise Street, Rotherhithe: an early nineteenth-century house converted to police use with an addition of the cell block in 1836. [London Metropolitan Archives].

constables attached to the magistrates' office, who continued to function separately. The principal officers under the Act were Justices of the Peace, retitled under the Metropolitan Police Act of 1829 as 'Commissioners of the Police of the Metropolis.' The two Commissioner posts were initially filled by Sir Richard Mayne, a barrister, and Colonel Charles Rowan who had served under Wellington at Waterloo. For the next hundred years men from the services were considered the right material for senior positions in the police force.

The third senior post was that of the Receiver. Under the 1829 legislation, he was empowered to 'make all such contracts and disbursements, as shall be necessary for purchasing or renting any land or buildings, or for the erecting, fitting up, furnishing or repairing buildings for use under the purposes of this Act'.[6] Clearly this role is crucial when investigating the design and erection of London's earliest purpose-built police buildings. The first Receiver was John Wray whose first task was to house the headquarters of the new police force. The premises had to be close to the Home Office, and the site chosen was a converted house, 4 Whitehall Place. It accommodated the two Commissioners and three clerks, and the Receiver and his two clerks. The total manpower of the new police force comprised eight superintendents, 20 inspectors, 85 sergeants, and 895 constables.

The main task facing the new force was to police the inner areas of the Metropolis which was initially divided into six divisions. Divisions A–F were formed in September 1829, with Divisions G–S designated in 1837. Each division had its head office converted from an existing building. The Covent Garden Division, for example, began its life in the old watch house in St Paul's churchyard, even re-using the cells underground.

CHARLES REEVES AND THE DEVELOPMENT OF THE NEW TYPE

As Receiver, Wray took over nearly 70 former watch houses which

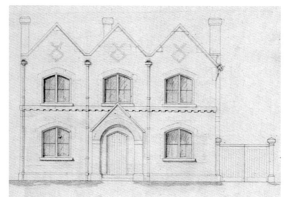

Fig. 3 Drawing of 1844 for a police station at South Mimms by Charles Reeves, the first Police Surveyor. [National Archives].

were graded according to size, locality and strategic importance. Divisional headquarters were broadly termed 'stations'; smaller buildings were known as 'station houses'. By the late 1830s the Commissioners and the Receiver were addressing the need for new buildings. The chief requirements were: a charge room, an office for the duty sergeant, quarters for single men as well as accommodation for an inspector or superintendent, and holding cells.

By 1840 it was clear that a separate department dedicated to providing new accommodation was needed, responsible for acquiring land and erecting purpose-built stations and courts. In 1842 the Surveyors' Department was established comprising a chief surveyor, an assistant surveyor, a clerk of works, and two office assistants, probably articled apprentices.

The first surveyor was Charles Reeves, born in 1815 at Fordingbridge, Hampshire. Previously he was articled to Annesley Voysey, the grandfather of Charles Annesley Voysey. Reeves and Voysey later formed a partnership which lasted until Voysey's death in 1847. Reeves subsequently went into partnership with Lewis Butcher until his own death in 1866. As a police surveyor he spent the most part of his working life designing and superintending the erection of 44 police stations in London, and following his appointment as architect to the county courts in 1847, 64 new court houses all over the country.

Reeves's first task was to acquire land and the Surveyors' Department records in the National Archives at Kew are full of such dealings. He looked for sites near or preferably on the main road, building access roads if necessary. Having found a suitable site he sought approval from Commissioner Sir Richard Mayne, and then from the Home Secretary to go ahead. Two of Reeves's earliest plans dating from the mid-1840s survive among the plans at Kew, for South Mimms and Twickenham, one in the Gothic style like a small vicarage of the period (**Fig. 3**); and one in the classical style (**Fig. 4**). The simple layout reflects the domestic nature of the buildings. They are of modest scale – two storeys high – with accommodation on the first floor

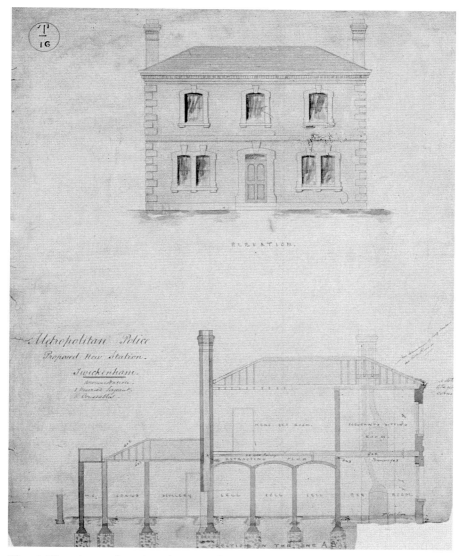

Fig. 4 Elevation and section drawings for a police station at Twickenham, 1847, by Charles Reeves. [National Archives].

for one married sergeant and one constable, with a sitting room. Only one ground floor room was for police business, the other was a day room for the sergeant's use and a kitchen. An interesting feature of the Twickenham station is that the cells were contained within the main building, below the police living quarters. In his later plans – from the 1850s onwards – Reeves placed

the cells at the rear of the main block, but the living arrangements remained substantially the same.

The 1850s and 1860s were a period of experimentation for Reeves as he sought ways of providing cells, office space and living accommodation in a compact and economical way which improved on the old watch houses. These, he observed, in a report to the Receiver in 1863, often had 'only one small room for police business, indifferent cells which open into the charge room, all unfit for purpose.' Constables were living half a mile from the station in private lodgings. On his requisition form, Reeves proposed a new station containing eleven rooms, including a day room, charge room, drying room, coal store, three water closets for the comfort of the officers, three cells and a separate stable block. Such provision became standard for a police station and in later years Reeves habitually encased these rooms in a small, square stock brick building with arched windows, prominent quoins and a minimum of stone dressings. Most of the stations were two storeys high with a central entrance. This formula stood Reeves in good stead when, after the mid-nineteenth century, there was a pressing need for more new stations to serve the needs of the expanding population.

In July 1857, the Home Secretary, Sir George Grey, prepared a Bill 'For Raising a Sum of Money for Building and Improving Stations of the Metropolitan Police'. Its introductory paragraph states that, 'whereas it has become necessary to build new stations for the Metropolitan Police, and as the expense of such building and improvement will exceed the amount defrayed out of the annual receipts applicable to the purpose of the Metropolitan Police, it is expedient that, towards defraying such expenses, a sum of sixty thousand pounds should be raised as hereinafter mentioned'.[7] The money was to be raised from Police rates in the Metropolitan District. The cost of a typical police station was then about £2,500, so allowing for the fact not all the money would be spent on new buildings, the erection of about fifteen new stations was certainly possible.

Charles Reeves had his formula ready and throughout London's high streets and suburban village centres his distinctive stations were erected. Surviving examples can be seen at Highgate, Kentish Town, Lewisham and Greenwich (**Fig. 5**). Highgate had some historical distinction as it was the first station to have a room set aside especially for the purpose of magistrates holding Petty Sessions; previously these had been held in a public house. As more money was made available by the Receiver, Reeves was able to build grander divisional headquarters in London and, as architect to the County Courts following the County Courts Act of 1846, court buildings such as the one at Rochester, of 1865. This is in the Gothic rather than the classical style, a more prevalent style for both courts and police stations outside London, often designed by the county architect. Reeves died in 1866 having devoted most of his working life to building police stations and courts.

THOMAS CHARLES SORBY

At the time of his death, Reeves's assistant was John Butler; however, the

Fig. 6 King's Cross Police Station, 1868-70, by T.C. Sorby. This fine Italianate building with its prominent royal coat of arms above the entrance accommodated 96 constables, two inspectors and two superintendents, with offices on the ground floor. [Author].

vacant Police Surveyorship was not given to Butler but to Thomas Charles Sorby in 1868. Sorby was born in Chevet in Yorkshire in 1836, and had been articled to Reeves, possibly from the late 1850s. His time in post was brief. He designed a police court in Lower Kennington Road and the handsome stable block at Rochester Row. However, in October of that year, 1868, an announcement was made in *The Times* stating that Sorby had accepted the post of Surveyor General to St George's Hospital, and he was compelled to give up the Police Surveyorship.[8] Sorby had built a few more police stations at the time of his resignation, including those at Vine Street and the divisional headquarters at Clerkenwell, for which special treatment was reserved. Here, features were made of the Italianate stone window dressings and the large royal arms above the entrance (**Fig. 6**).

One might expect the choice of the classical style to have been deliberate – a kind of *architecture parlante*, perhaps taking its cue from the dignity and gravitas associated, for example, with George Dance the Younger's weighty Piranesian exterior of Newgate prison. However, no documentary evidence has been discovered to express thoughts of this nature, the issues of concern for the police surveyors being the more practical matters of decent and sufficient accommodation and, around 1867 (the time of the Irish Fenian attacks on Clerkenwell prison), the issue of security, with the need to fortify central stations with bullet-proof iron shutters. The question of style does not emerge as an issue or a matter of public debate until the building of New Scotland Yard in the late 1880s.

FREDERICK CAIGER AND THE SANITATION REPORT.

Upon Sorby's resignation the Home Secretary appointed Sorby's deputy Frederick Caiger as Chief Surveyor, and John Butler was appointed Deputy Surveyor. Caiger's salary was £500 per annum, and Butler's was £300, slightly more than senior police officers. Caiger had been a pupil of Thomas Hellyer, an architect whose practice was focused on the production of schools, churches and vicarages on the Isle of Wight.[9] His task was basically to carry on Reeves's work and in the same manner, with repairs and alterations being the priority rather than new buildings.

In 1881 a case of diphtheria was recorded at Rotherhithe police station, and an investigation into causes snowballed into an inquiry into the general state of sanitation in police stations. This was a period of interest in sanitation in domestic housing generally, and a police station was certainly among the most heavily 'lived in' buildings of the period. A vivid account of an evening in Leman Street police station in Whitechapel by Thomas Archer in 1865 described how 'the new arrival [in the cell] asks for some water, and is supplied with a tin full, and though the bench on which he lies is hard, and the wooden block which forms the pillow uninviting, the cell itself is clean and well ventilated, as it need be, since before morning it may receive four or five other inmates.'[10]

The surgeons' report to the Sanitary Committee was hard-hitting, highlighting problems such as badly-trapped drains, drinking water that came from the same supply which served the lavatory cisterns, bad ventilation exacerbating damp, small, overcrowded cells and no sick rooms. One of the District Surgeons wanted to see a separate medical room provided in all new police stations. At the moment, he reported, people are kept in the charge room in unseemly circumstances. He described a scene he had witnessed where a man was having his head bandaged 'while a female in the dock who had injured him, half tipsy, and several witnesses and police officers looked on.' The report concluded: 'These are some of the defects existing in a large number of our London police stations. They would not be suffered to exist for a day in any of our prisons'.[11]

Caiger's response drew attention to the difficulty of converting domestic residences to police use; and the fact that there was no consensus from the 'Men of Science' on what constituted a good, effective system of drainage. He emphasised instead his ideas on improved cells for containing city criminals:

> The majority of prisoners when put into Metropolitan cells are under the influence of drink and passion, not infrequently bordering on madness. In this state, mischief, suicide or a desire to escape is the first thing contemplated. Consequently, the facility to do any of these things is to be guarded against. My experience has led me to conclude that everything in the way of glass, however thick in substance, and iron ventilators, must be placed beyond their reach. With these facts in view, the cells so constructed offer the smallest possible facility for prisoners committing suicide or effecting their escape.[12]

He added that his plans for police cells had been approved by Sir Joshua Jebb, late Inspector General of Prisons.

Yet for all his efforts, Caiger did not convince the authorities. He was asked to set about improving sanitary arrangements at police stations straight away, and before the end of the year his assistant and Deputy Surveyor John Butler had been appointed Surveyor to the Metropolitan Police in his stead. It seems that Caiger was dismissed. Nevertheless, a number of stations were designed and built by Caiger in the 1870s, particularly between 1874–7, a good number in the outer suburbs such as Isleworth, Ealing and Enfield. They were solid, decent, classical buildings in the Reeves mould though longer and deeper than the earlier prototypes. Caiger can also be credited with the uniquely Gothic Kensington Police Station erected in 1873 adjacent to Sir George Gilbert Scott's church of St Mary Abbots, 1868–72 (**Fig. 7**). Objections had been raised, reported *The Builder*, on the grounds that it would 'mar the effect of the edifice adjoining.' A compromise was reached: 'To meet such objections, it was decided that, in its architectural design and character, the building should present a more ornamental appearance than structures of this nature usually do, and be made to harmonise as far as possible with its ornamental Gothic neighbour'.[13]

JOHN BUTLER AND THE EXPANSION OF POLICE STATIONS AND SECTION HOUSES IN LONDON, 1881-1895.

John Butler trained with several architects including William White, before setting up his own practice in 1862. His early work listed in his RIBA fellowship nomination papers were 'villas in Wandsworth, Camberwell and West Hampstead and the vestry hall at St Clement Danes'. From 1857, the year of the Police Bill, Butler had been clerk of works under Reeves, and had assisted him on plans for the early new stations; with around 25 years experience he was well qualified to succeed Caiger to the Surveyorship in 1881.

Butler's first task was to refurbish existing stations by implementing the health inspectors' recommendations. As well as emphasising drainage, sanitation

Fig. 7 Kensington Police Station, 1872-3, by Frederick Caiger, in a Gothic Revival style to respect that of its neighbour, the church of St Mary Abbots, which had only recently been completed to the designs of George Gilbert Scott, 1868-72. [Author].

Fig. 8 Design for a section house at Shepherd's Bush by John Butler, 1883, showing the single-storey link between the section house and the office. [National Archives].

and overcrowding, the report of the Sanitary Committee recommended that the administrative block of a station should be separate from the residential block or 'section house', 'to prevent interference with the freedom and privacy of resident officers, and to make their quarters more like a home'.[14] Such a separation can be seen at Shepherd's Bush of 1883, where the two blocks were linked by a single-storey corridor (**Fig. 8**).

In more constricted urban sites section houses and station were combined – sometimes up to six storeys high – and contained dormitories, a recreation room, library, kitchen and a room for 'storing muddy boots.' The size of the particularly large Leman Street station in Whitechapel designed in 1890 was in direct response to the outcry caused by Jack the Ripper murders in 1887-8, and the generally high level of East End crime.

Contemporary reports on living in section houses vary in evaluation. Those attached to the principal London stations were popular with unmarried men who, according to Charles Booth's survey on the police of 1894, liked 'the more lively central parts, while married men preferred the suburban district'.[15] Not all single men were housed in section houses; many found accommodation in what Booth described as 'better class block dwellings.' This seems to have been the case at Charing Cross, where 48 of the 156 families were those of police officers. In his survey Booth concluded that, in section houses, 'the accommodation is rather better than that provided for soldiers in barracks…but refinements are lacking'.[16]

This view was endorsed by a contemporary letter to the *Police Review and Parade Gossip* headed 'Section House mismanagement and discomforts.' Among the list of complaints were 'the petty tyranny which prevails…noise coming from men returning from night duty, and confinement indoors for hours in anticipation of action during strikes and riots for which neither payment nor time off is given in return'.[17] The concentration of large numbers of officers in one area was obviously desirable from a police point of view. The same journal, announcing the opening of a new section house in Stoke Newington, stated that it was part of a scheme introduced by the Commissioner to 'increase the efficiency of the Metropolitan Police ... at Stoke Newington there will be practically day and night a reserve of fifty men ready for an emergency'.[18]

THE 1880s: POLITICAL UNREST AND NEW SCOTLAND YARD.

Police stations increased from the late 1880s; partly due to increased crime in the East End, but also in consequence of political activity in central London. In 1883 the Irish Fenians renewed their attacks, and dynamited the office of *The Times*, the local government office in Whitehall, and the Scotland Yard Police headquarters at 4 Whitehall Place. In February 1886 rival meetings held in Trafalgar Square between the unemployed and members of Hyndman's Social Democratic Federation led to rioting which the police could not control. The ensuing inquiry report highlighted the absence of co-ordination from the senior ranks, the poor communication between stations, and sheer lack of manpower. Commissioner James Monro explained the gravity of the situation: 'Of a total complement of 14,000 men, only 9,000 were on duty at any one time, covering an area of 700 square miles from Colney Heath to Tadworth Heath, from Lark Hall in Essex to Staines Moor in Middlesex'.[19] This was a huge increase in the original area of the Metropolitan Police District, a six-mile radius from Charing Cross. There had been a massive increase in population, buildings and traffic, particularly in the suburbs. Other exacerbating factors were more constables being deployed in the East End and not being replaced, and political meetings in Hyde Park particularly on Sundays.

The report led Home Secretary Matthews to consent to 1,000 men being recruited over the following year, an increase of 500%. Clearly more stations would be needed to accommodate them. The Metropolitan Police Act of 1886 empowered the Receiver to raise £200,000 to buy land and erect new stations. John Butler also set about acquiring more land for extending existing stations, as that on the Isle of Dogs. The funding was increased the following year with the passing of another Act allowing the Receiver 'to provide, by building a central office and such police stations, offices, houses and buildings as are required by the Metropolitan Police Force and to improve, enlarge and fit up offices, stations etc'.[20] This brought the total to £500,000.

The 'central office' referred to in the Act was to be the New Scotland Yard. The original headquarters at 4 Whitehall Place had long been too small. *The Times* of May 1890 declared: 'Innumerable books are piled up on staircases, so that they are almost impassable, piles of clothing, saddles and horse furniture, blankets, are heaped up in little garrets in a state of what, outside Scotland Yard, would be called hopeless confusion'.[21]

In 1877 Commissioner Henderson had considered converting Francis

Fowler's unfinished 'Grand National Opera House' on the Victoria Embankment for police use, but nothing came of this. This site was eventually cleared in 1881 and the Receiver, Alfred Richard Pennefather, bought it for £186,000. Butler began designing the new headquarters, but Pennefather was eventually successful in persuading the Mr Matthews, the newly-appointed Home Secretary, that a major building on such a conspicuous site required an architect of the highest public reputation, and in 1887 Richard Norman Shaw was brought in to take over.

Shaw's first designs were exhibited at the Royal Academy in May 1887 which *The Builder* described as:

> an exceedingly solid-looking building, the lower two storeys of stone, the upper of brick, the latter portion containing the principal window tiers, which are Classical in treatment, with architraves and pediments to the lower ones and heavy keystones to the upper ones...The building as shown here does not display much of its architect's play of fancy, perhaps considered out of place in a building of this class; but it is a capital piece of solid, unpretentious architecture, and it is gratifying to find the authorities going to an architect like Mr Shaw for such a

Fig. 9 New Scotland Yard, North Building by Richard Norman Shaw, 1887–90 [The Victorian Society].

building instead of inflicting official architecture upon us.[22]

After the bombing of Old Scotland Yard, it was essential that the new building should look impregnable so the lower floors were faced with granite, quarried from Dartmoor by convicts. Cheap Portland stone from state-owned quarries was also used, although red brick was the dominant material. The building was planned as an open square, with corridors generally facing the inner court. When the Commissioner took up residence in 1890 he was housed in the top room overlooking the river, with the reception rooms for members of the public on the ground floor (**Fig. 9**).[23]

Although side-lined from the design of the police headquarters, the Police Surveyor John Butler continued designing police stations and section houses all over London. He had always made use of decorative architectural features in his stations – gables at Shepherd's Bush (1882), Venetian windows at Leman Street (1890), *oeil de boeuf* windows at Fulham (1886) and prominent Butterfieldian chimneys at Trinity Road, Tooting (1886), but a distinct Shavian influence can be seen in stations after 1890. Most conspicuous is the use of red brick and stone banding, outsized pedimented gables and projecting windows, as at Blackwall station built in 1893 on the Isle of Dogs (**Fig. 10**). This station is compact and thoughtful, as neat as the police station boat *The Royalty* which it replaced, and it epitomises John Butler's skill as a planner of police buildings. Blackwall station straddles a dock for police boats, with a charge room, office and cell accommodation on the ground floor, living quarters for four married men above, and a special room for drying wet clothes.

Fig. 11 Cannon Row Police Station by John Dixon Butler, 1900–2. [London Metropolitan Archives].

POLICE STATIONS AND MAGISTRATES' COURTS BY JOHN DIXON BUTLER

By 1895, when he resigned, John Butler had erected twenty new stations with money raised under the Police Acts of 1886 and 1887. It was time to pass the torch on to his son, John Dixon Butler. The younger Butler was appointed Architect and Surveyor to the Metropolitan Police in October 1895. He was well qualified for the job. He was elected a fellow of the RIBA in 1906 and his nomination papers state that he was articled to his father, John Butler between 1877 and 1881. He also studied with Professor Hayter-Lewis at University College, and was a member of the Architectural Association from 1880. After the standard sketching tour of cathedrals and abbeys in Northern France, Dixon Butler began by laying out the estate and houses at Grosvenor Place for Lord Cathcart. In his capacity as architect to the Kensington Church Education Board he built St Matthew's school and St James Norlands school in Kensington, and supervised alterations at 45 Kensington Square for a solicitor called Alexander Nelson Radcliffe. Radcliffe's father-in-law was the Commissioner Sir Edward Bradford, so John Dixon Butler probably benefited from such a high-ranking connection.

On appointment Dixon Butler's task was to assist Norman Shaw in the completion of New Scotland Yard and a new police station adjacent to the site at Cannon Row. Although credited to Dixon Butler in the published design, the hand of Shaw is evident in the treatment of the exterior: red brick and stone banding, the hooded dormer breaking through the cornice line and the tall, prominent chimneys (**Fig. 11**).

The influence was not just one way. An interesting exchange of architectural ideas was taking place between the celebrated architect and the man who knew a good deal about planning police stations through his long apprenticeship with his father; this can be seen at Kentish Town police station in Holmes Road. Shaw had been asked a few years earlier, in 1891, to design a new police station as the headquarters of Y Division, just off the busy Kentish Town Road (**Fig. 12**). Reeves's old station at the junction of Fortess Road and Kentish Town Road was a minnow in comparison. The new station at Holmes Road was not completed until 1896, and had vastly exceeded its estimate, costing £12,500 instead of the budget of £8,000. In defence, Shaw's champion, Richard Pennefather, explained to the Commissioner the reason, and the value of Shaw's involvement, which had been his personal choice:

> The new station at Kentish Town has been designed by Norman Shaw, and it is perhaps on this account that it has been slightly more expensive than had it been designed by Mr Butler, as Mr Shaw goes in for rather greater strength in construction than we should adopt, and he has allowed the men a greater cubic capacity. Here are good points, even if they cost a little more money … I consider that it will be of very great advantage to the Service to have the experience of one of the leading architects of the day in the construction of a police station, and it will at any rate show that the work designed in this department is designed on economical lines.[24]

The Commissioner, it seems, was not convinced and commented that Shaw's rebuilding of Walton Street police station had also exceeded its estimate. The Receiver replied, 'the expense was due to Norman Shaw the architect not knowing much about police requirements, and employing a quantity surveyor who did not know much either. As the employment of Mr Shaw on these two stations was exceptional, similar cost is not likely to be incurred

Fig. 12 Holmes Road Police Station, Kentish Town, designed in 1891, built 1894-6 by Richard Norman Shaw. [Author].

148

again'.[25] Both these buildings were well within the established tradition of the neighbourhood police station design on the exterior, and particularly in the planning of the arrangement of the cells to the side, offices above, and stable yard behind. If Shaw took a degree of plainness from the police station tradition as well as functional planning, the new surveyor John Dixon Butler, like his father, saw the aesthetic possibilities of Shaw's style at Scotland Yard. A good example of this is Dixon Butler's 1900 design for Highgate police station in the Queen Anne style to replace one by Charles Reeves. Ironically, Reeves's station survives; the later one does not. Dixon Butler's station was to house administrative offices, three single cells and one association cell – a larger cell to contain people detained on the same charge. Living quarters were provided for one married sergeant and 16 single men. Once again the estimate of £6,500 was exceeded by £2,000; even the official Police Surveyor could not always come in on budget!

London's late Victorian and Edwardian suburbs are still rich in police stations and section houses designed by John Dixon Butler, with good examples at Clapton, Harrow Road, Hampstead, Newham and Wapping. His body of work displays a wonderful range of styles, from the handsome, Mackintosh-inspired section house at Beak Street of 1909, to the small suburban stations such as Sutton, of the same date, which was praised by *The Builder* for 'its simple and sensible style, without useless or pretentious ornament'.[26]

Butler's versatility in police station design can be seen in two stations of 1913: Kew and Tottenham. Whereas Kew is a small three-storey cottage style building, domestic and cosy (**Fig. 13**), Tottenham High Road station, described on the drawings as a 'first class town police station', ten bays wide and three storeys high, with look-out round bays at the corner, is austere and intimidating (**Fig. 14**). Kew was to house only two married sergeants and four constables; Tottenham housed 60 single men in dormitories which occupied the whole of the second and third floors. Cells at Kew are out of sight; those at Tottenham are prominent, lining the side elevation to Chestnut Road. The drawings for the elevations and plans of Tottenham police station are delicately tinted in watercolour with fastidious pencil details of cornices and brackets; of all the police surveyors John Dixon Butler was the nearest to an art-architect.

After 1898 the responsibility for court design returned to the Metropolitan Police Authority from the Office of Works. The Receiver was empowered to raise £700,000 for the new buildings, with specific entrances and rooms for magistrates, and separate waiting areas for the public, witnesses and the accused. The advantage of a court next to the police station is clear: the ease of transfer of prisoners from cells to dock. The nine magistrates' courts built by Butler from 1903–13 comprise his finest achievement. They are architecturally exuberant, even flamboyant; a far cry from the rather bleak utilitarianism of

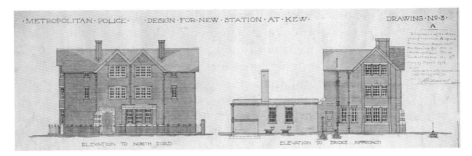

Fig. 13 Drawing for Kew Police Station by John Dixon Butler, 1913. [National Archives].

Reeve's buildings. Notable examples are at Old Street in Shoreditch which combined a police station and court; Tooley Street and King's Cross (**Fig. 15**). All individually designed, they share beautiful and distinctive features: high-quality red brickwork and stone dressings; oversized pediments, sometimes broken in a fruity Edwardian Baroque fashion; giant *oeil de boeuf* windows; swollen porch brackets flanking the principal entrances; and robust surrounding cast-iron railings with a distinctive design.

Dixon Butler also enlarged existing police stations. He added an extra storey and new cells to Caiger's Commercial Street station in 1905; he incorporated Reeves's Gothic elevation at Paddington into a five-bay extension in 1913; he created an open area to ease congestion between cells at Marylebone Lane. Common additions in the early 1900s comprised a dedicated medical room (finally!), telegraph rooms and extended CID offices, which reflected the increased workload in this department since its foundation in 1842. Within the police compound he made provision for shelters for ambulance litters,

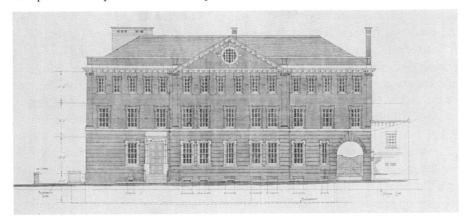

Fig. 14 Drawing for Tottenham Police Station, John Dixon Butler, 1913. [National Archives].

Fig. 15 King's Cross Magistrates' Court by John Dixon Butler, 1903-6. This building shows a number of features typical of Dixon Butler's London courts: high-quality red brick with Portland stone dressings, *oeil de boeuf* windows, swollen porch brackets, and a giant semi-circular Portland stone pediment over the entrance. [Author].

bicycle sheds, a parade ground, and garages for motors that began to replace stable blocks.

John Dixon Butler worked right up to his death in November 1920. He had completed over 200 police buildings, including nine courts, of high architectural quality, and a vast improvement in facilities from the early days of Reeves's work. Sadly only around 58 stations are known to survive, of which 19 are listed, as well as all nine courts. A number have been successfully converted to new use.

CONCLUSION

The form of the Metropolitan police station emerged in the 1840s as a result of the need to link together the functions of crime detection, holding suspects, and of arrest and charge, that is, the initial stage in the judicial process for which the Home Secretary was responsible. The location, planning and appearance of the stations were the responsibility of the Police Surveyors' Department founded in 1842, directed by the Chief Surveyor. The principal features housed within the police compound were: the main station accommodating a front office on the ground floor for the reception of public; a charge room; superintendent's office; living quarters for constables either on the upper storeys of the main building or in a separate residential block or 'section house'; a cell block attached at the rear of the main building; a parade ground enclosed by a high wall; provision for stables and, later, police cars. The architectural style evolved from a severe classicism dominant from 1842 until 1881, through a Queen Anne influence inspired by Richard Norman Shaw and introduced into standard police buildings by John Butler, then creatively developed in the Edwardian period by John Dixon Butler. Throughout the period the style was not codified but left to the discretion and ability of the

Police Surveyor, each having his own identifiable interpretation.

In 1842 the Metropolitan Police Surveyor's Department, with a staff of four or five, was finding sites and erecting stations for £2,500 a building. By 1920 the average cost of stations and the court buildings was more like £35,000. Looking at the output of each Surveyor active between 1842 and 1920, Reeves had built 44 stations; Sorby, 10; Caiger, 11; John Butler, 20; and John Dixon Butler, over 200 police stations, section houses and courts. It was a remarkable achievement.

Notes

1. The focus here is on the police stations and the magistrates' courts designed by the Police Surveyor, rather than on the Assize, Crown, County and Sessions courts – which is a rather different, more complex subject of study. *See* Clare Graham, *Ordering Law: the Architectural and Social History of the English Law Court to 1914*, Farnham, 2003. Allan Brodie, Gary Winter and Stephen Porter, 'The Law Court 1800-2000', English Heritage Report, 2001.
2. 34 Edw III, c.1.
3. 32 Geo.III, c.53.
4. *The Public Advertiser*, 1793.
5. Metropolitan Police Act 19 June 1829, Geo.IV, c.44.
6. Ibid.
7. Metropolitan Police Act 6 July 1857, 20 & 21 Vict. c. 64.
8. RIBA biography file for T.C. Sorby.
9. *Architects', Engineers' and Building Trades Directory*, 1868, pp. 104, 137.
10. Thomas Archer, *The Pauper, the Thief and the Convict,* London, 1865, p. 104.
11. National Archives, MEPO 5/64, Report of the Sanitary Committee, 1881.
12. National Archives, MEPO 5/64/545.
13. *The Builder*, 21 February 1874, p.160.
14. National Archives, MEPO 5/64, Report of the Sanitary Committee, 1881.
15. Charles Booth, *A Life and Labour of the People*, 2nd ser., vol. 4, London, 1903, p. 47.
16. Ibid., p. 535.
17. *Police Review and Parade Gossip*, 1894.
18. Ibid.
19. Annual Report from the Commissioners of the Police to the Secretary of State for the Home Department, 1887.
20. Metropolitan Police Act 4 June 1886, 49 Vict. c. 22.
21. *The Times*, 3 May 1890, p. 6.
22. *The Builder,* 21 May 1887, p. 760.
23. Susan Beattie, 'New Scotland Yard', *Architectural History*, 15, 1972, pp. 68–81.
24. National Archives, HO/45/A46538, correspondence re Kentish Town police station, 1896.
25. Ibid.
26. *The Builder*, 6 March 1909, p. 282.

8 The Stamp of Official Architecture: English Post Offices

ROBERT HRADSKY

The Post Office has been in decline for so long, it is perhaps hard to imagine that it was once a dynamic, thriving and highly profitable organisation. In fact, the unstoppable growth of the postal network over the course of the nineteenth century is one of the great success stories of Victorian Britain. From modest beginnings it grew into a vast machine of great complexity and efficiency. By the early twentieth century, when the Post Office was at the peak of its prosperity, it could boast proud public buildings in all the principal towns and cities, the largest of which were major civic landmarks. The total number of post offices grew from 4,028 in 1840 to 24,354 in 1913. Throughout our period, the Post Office operated as a government department; no other department of state had a greater presence in all parts of the country. Indeed, the buildings and uniformed employees of the Post Office were the most tangible representations of government in the lives of ordinary people. This chapter explores the form that representation took, as manifested in the purpose-built post office, examples of which were built all over the country in the years down to the First World War.

BEGINNINGS

By the time the first specialist post office buildings were erected, a postal network of sorts had already existed for some three hundred years. As early as 1516, Henry VIII appointed his own Master of Posts, supported by postmasters at stages along the main routes from London. This system was originally intended solely for the private use of government. However, the wider benefits of secure and reliable communication were obvious and by the early seventeenth century it had evolved into a nascent public amenity, eventually confirmed by Acts of 1657 and 1660, which set down the postal rates to be charged.[1] By the eighteenth century it was firmly established as a government department, headed by Postmasters General – one Whig and one Tory. Eventually this became a single appointment, made by whichever party was in power. Compared with other offices of state, the office of Postmaster

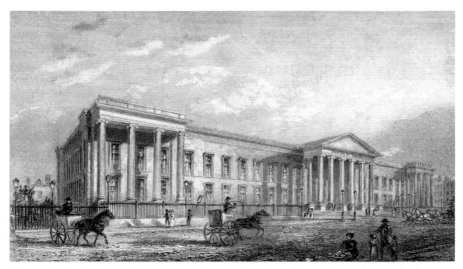

Fig. 1 Sir Robert Smirke's General Post Office, London, 1825–9 (demolished 1912). A nineteenth-century engraving of England's first purpose-built post office, showing mail coaches. [J. Mason, *Youth's Instruction*, London, 1830].

General was not the most glamorous position, but it carried with it the patronage of appointing postmasters throughout the country.

Throughout the early history of the Post Office the local postmaster was responsible for providing the necessary facilities, the rent of which would be taken into account in fixing his allowance. The earliest post offices were not buildings in their own right, but mere collection points within shops or other buildings where the postal activity was limited to the posting of letters. There was, therefore, no need to provide a space for face-to-face transactions. Nonetheless, in country areas, these modest receiving houses must have been foci of village life. Certainly, this is how they are portrayed in Jane Austen's *Emma* of 1815 – 'the post-office is a wonderful establishment' – and in E.V. Rippingille's painting *A Country Post Office* in 1819, which is thronged with villagers from all walks of life.

Even the national headquarters of the Post Office occupied makeshift accommodation in London until well into the nineteenth century. Around 1678 the Post Office moved from Threadneedle Street to an old house in Lombard Street. Making the alterations to this building probably constituted the principal workload of both J. T. Groves (*c.*1761-1811) and Joseph Kay (1775-1847) in their successive positions as architects to the Post Office. There were moves toward providing a new London facility in 1814, but Kay's designs remained unexecuted due to bureaucratic vacillation. In the event, Kay's Edinburgh Post Office (1818-19) became Britain's first purpose-built facility.

Eventually, the design by Sir Robert Smirke (1780-1867) for the London General Post Office on a new site in St Martin's le Grand was accepted. Built in 1825-9, it thus became the first purpose-built post office in England (**Fig. 1**). It was acclaimed in its time and is well known today as one of the principal landmarks in the history of the Greek Revival. Its austere classicism can also be said to have set the tone for post office design up until the 1880s.

Few purpose-built post offices survive from the period 1840 to 1860, but it seems likely that conservative Greek Revival designs were common, such as that designed for Nottingham by the city's Corporation Surveyor H. M. Wood (*c.*1847, demolished). In Devonport, a group of shareholders erected a handsome late classical post office (1850: **Fig. 2**) that was designed by George Wightwick (1802–72), the leading architect in the western counties.

REFORM

In the provinces, the burden on postmasters to provide adequate facilities increased as the postal service became ever more popular. The problem was more acute in larger towns with higher land values, so that the Post Office often had to step in to lease the building or pay for the erection of a new one. This became increasingly necessary after 1840, with the inauguration of

Fig. 2 Devonport Post Office, 1850 (demolished 1945), by George Wightwick. Note the caduceus in the centre, a common post office motif. The building was later acquired and altered by the Office of Works. [A contemporary engraving].

the penny post under the reforms associated with Rowland Hill. Hill had no special interest in architecture, but the introduction of a uniform rate of pre-payment for letters had major repercussions for the buildings of the Post Office. Hill's prediction that the penny post would dramatically increase people's use of the system was more than fulfilled. Thanks to the development of postal services, by 1859 93% of letters were being delivered free of any additional charge.[2] Just before Hill's reforms the average number of letters sent was three per person per year; by 1875 it was 31.[3] The mounting pressure this put on Britain's post office network came to a head in the late 1850s, when a survey was ordered of all the post offices in large towns.

In 1857 an exhaustive questionnaire was sent to postmasters throughout the provinces. Fifty-nine questions ranged from the fine details of administration to more prosaic concerns such as whether the letter box was fixed to the building properly. Regarding the buildings, it asked 'is the post office conveniently situated and of sufficient size for the performance of all the duties' with 'proper shelter and accommodation provided for the public?' Too many replies were negative, and furnishings in particular were found to be inadequate. The question of updating furnishings was complicated by ownership, as a departmental memo makes clear: 'At Ipswich, Norwich and other places the fittings belong to the Department while at Cambridge and elsewhere they are the property of the Postmaster and in other instances I believe they belong to the landlord.' There were heated arguments within the department over how to deal with the inadequacy of the post offices that it had little control over. The feeling within the Post Office seems to have been that the local postmasters were not keeping up with the vision of an expanding organisation. So, at considerable expense, the Department bit the bullet and took much greater control of all post offices.[4]

OFFICE OF WORKS

From 1858 the official provision of premises was taken over by the Government's Office of Works, which meant that salaried public architects came to the fore in the design of new post office buildings. The justification for the involvement of the Office of Works was that it could provide consistent professional expertise across the whole country, and that major post offices were granted the same status as other government buildings such as courthouses. Inevitably, the exchange of information between the Post Office and Office of Works became intensely bureaucratic, and even more so when the Treasury was involved. The way post offices were categorised is complicated enough. Those designed by the Office of Works were labelled Crown Office Class I, as opposed to the lesser Class II offices which were usually designed by local architects. To add further confusion, these labels correspond only loosely with the three main categories of post office:

Head post office: usually designated a Crown Office Class I, designed and maintained by the Office of Works.
Branch post office: designated a Crown Office Class II, usually leased and maintained by the Post Office.
Sub post office: sometimes treated like a Crown Office Class II but often a shop incorporating a post office, a premises owned or leased by the shopkeeper.[5]

Regardless of how post offices were ranked and administered, their sheer number was immensely impressive. The Postmaster General reported their growth as follows:

1855: 920 head offices in larger towns and 9,578 smaller sub-offices;
1913: 1,098 offices in larger towns and 23,256 sub-offices.[6]

The Office of Works looked after the buildings for which it was responsible by using a staff of architects, surveyors and engineers based mainly in London but with some staff in the regions. Post offices represented 43 per cent of its overall workload, so it was fiercely resistant to claims that the Post Office should look after all its own buildings.[7] Meanwhile, the Post Office had its own organisation for dealing with the buildings of a lesser kind (Class II and below) which fell within its remit. They were managed by Surveyors, career

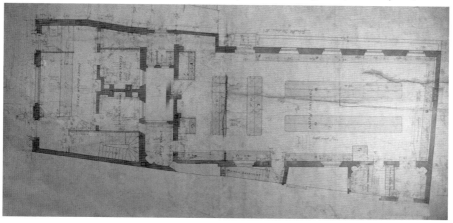

Fig. 3 North Eastern District Post Office, London, 1859-60 (demolished), James Williams of HM Office of Works, illustrating the standard post office plan form. [National Archives].

bureaucrats like Anthony Trollope who had no specific training in architecture or building construction.

ROMAN RENAISSANCE

In 1858 James Williams (1824-92) of the Office of Works was appointed as architect in charge of post offices. It was probably Williams who established what came to be the standard form of a post office: a main block incorporating a public office on the ground floor with the postmaster's living quarters above, adjoining to the rear a single-storey top-lit sorting office. Ancillary spaces included clerks' rooms and public retiring rooms. Drawings for the London North Eastern District Post Office in Bethnal Green of around 1860 show that this formula was already in place by 1859 (**Fig. 3**).[8] An early surviving example of this type from 1863 can be found in Lowther Street, Carlisle. Though this was the preferred model, on constrained sites the sorting office was sometimes located above the public office, as in Putney High Street (*c.*1873), or alongside, as in Market Street, Wakefield (1876, **Fig. 4**).[9] This basic plan form proved so successful in its ability to accommodate later extensions that it was used largely unchanged through to the 1950s.

Stylistically, Williams was unadventurous, though astonishingly consistent. He worked in a severe Roman Renaissance style that remained constant throughout his post office career. The crisply cut ornament of his offices (and of those designed under his direction) came from a limited palette of favourite motifs. These include attenuated triglyph brackets for doors or windows and a slim stringcourse decorated with a Greek key-fret or guilloche pattern. These can still be seen in several surviving examples, including Small Street, Bristol (1867, with later extensions), Victoria Street, Derby (*c.*1869), Regent Street, Barnsley (1881) and Bedford Street, London (1883-4, **Fig. 5**), all with subtle differences in the detailing. They have a strong rectilinear character that amounts to a Roman version of Smirke's Greek neoclassicism. It is easy to imagine how this ordered, handsome and dignified aesthetic might have been deemed appropriate for the public face of a government department.

Despite the consistency of the Office of Works' output under Williams, it did not add up to a distinctive house style. It is debatable whether the Williams post offices would have been readily identifiable amongst the many classical banks and other commercial premises of the time. This is, to an extent, borne out by the comments of the historian William Lewins, who in 1862 remarked that the head post office in a provincial town 'is metamorphosed into quite a grand establishment' appearing not unlike a 'first-class bank'.[10] Furthermore, despite the refinement of Williams' detail, he was at a loss with larger buildings, as was evident in the ponderous elevations of the West Range, General Post Office, London (1869-73, dem. 1967). A more significant achievement was the Head Post Office in Newcastle (1871-4) opposite St Nicholas's Cathedral, which achieves considerable grandeur through the use of superimposed giant orders.

OUTSIDERS

The Class II Crown Offices designed by local architects were, predictably, much more varied, both in plan and, especially, elevation, their designers being given free rein. They were often quite exuberant, such as a festive Queen Anne design in Knutsford, Cheshire (1886, demolished), a free Romanesque one in Fore Street, Hertford (1890), and a Gothic Revival office in Abbey Place,

Fig. 5 Bedford Street Post Office, London, 1883-4, by James Williams, illustrating the Roman Renaissance style employed between 1858 and 1884. [Alan Baxter].

Fig. 6 Ipswich Post Office, *c.*1880, by John Johnson. Selected in a competition, this is one of the most decorative post offices to survive. [*The Builder*, 12 June 1880, p. 735].

Thorney, Cambridgeshire (*c.*1860–70), the latter a picturesquely massed design attributed to that rogue architect S. S. Teulon. One of the most lavish examples to survive is John Johnson's Ipswich (*c.*1880), a florid free Renaissance design selected in a competition presided over by Charles Barry (**Fig. 6**).[11] Erected on a prominent site adjacent to the Town Hall, it illustrates well how post offices could become marked expressions of civic pride. After about 1880 many Crown II offices were in a Gothic Revival idiom, though smaller, more economically built facilities continued in a vernacular classical vein, such as that at South Embankment, Dartmouth (1888–9).

Fig. 7 Oxford Post Office, 1879, by E. G. Rivers of HM Office of Works. The two left bays were added about 1903 when the tower was extended upwards. [Alan Baxter].

Fig. 8 Croydon Post Office, *c.*1894, by Henry Tanner of HM Office of Works. Designed in an English Renaissance style, it had a caretaker's apartment on the top floor. [National Archives].

FORGING AHEAD

Before James Williams retired, the Office of Works began to deviate from classical sobriety with a number of Gothic Revival post offices designed by Edward George Rivers. These included St Aldate's, Oxford (1879, **Fig. 7**), Broad Street, Hereford (*c.*1881) and Plymouth (1885, demolished). Though not particularly spirited designs, they were indicative of things to come, for the output of the Office was to become far more eclectic under Henry Tanner (1849-1935), who in 1884 replaced Williams as head architect for post offices. Some of Tanner's earlier designs were in a Gothic Revival style akin to the work of Alfred Waterhouse, such as Commercial Street, Halifax (1886), though he came to prefer an English or Northern Renaissance style, used both on the smaller scale, as at High Street, Croydon (*c.*1894, **Fig. 8**)[12] or Dame Alice Street, Bedford (*c.*1897),[13] and on a large scale, as at Bradford (*c.*1887, **Fig. 9**), Leeds (1892-6) and Nottingham (1895-8). These palatial facilities, often symmetrically grouped with a lively skyline, placed the Post Office at the very heart of civic life.

Though post offices became more eclectic stylistically under Tanner in line with national trends, his chief concern was with technical improvements regarding planning and construction. In 1870 the Post Office had taken over the telegraph, an additional function with its own requirements. In its wake came other services – the parcel post, which started in 1883, and the gradual

Fig. 9 Bradford Post Office, *c.*1887, by Henry Tanner. Larger facilities were designed as grand civic gestures. [Early twentieth-century postcard: author's collection].

acquisition of private telephone companies, which culminated in telephones becoming a Post Office monopoly in 1912.[14] The staffing of these services meant a huge increase in the Post Office workforce, from nearly 100,000 in 1885 to 250,000 in 1914. Women were about a quarter of the workforce, employed mainly as counter clerks, telegraphists and telephone operators. The expanding role of the Post Office had major implications for the design of its buildings; what had once been a facility for the receipt and despatch of letters became something much more complex, with a separate telegraph instrument room and facilities for women clerks and telegram boys. When a telephone exchange was provided in the same building, the floorplan increased yet further. The public was still confined to only one part of the building, the public office on the ground floor, though it became increasingly difficult to fit all the services into a logical plan within a typical urban site.

Through Tanner's influence, plan forms and interior layout became increasingly standardized, and yet always adaptable to awkward sites. In general, he introduced greater rigour into the design of post offices and, unlike Williams, attained a high profile within the architectural profession. Craftsmanship was of the highest order, with every finish rigorously specified in the builder's contracts. In this way, the conduct of the Office of Works under Tanner is indicative of the growing professionalism of architecture in the late Victorian period.

MATERIAL INTERESTS

Tanner had a particular interest in construction, and was an early advocate of reinforced concrete framing, on which he chaired a committee in 1907.[15] He seized upon a loophole that exempted the Office of Works from the usual building controls, which restricted the use of the new technology. Tanner used the flagship King Edward Buildings at the General Post Office, London (1907-10), to experiment with reinforced concrete on the grandest scale (**Fig. 10**). The concrete framing was mostly concealed by Portland stone elevations in Tanner's usual Renaissance revival mode, though it was left exposed on the great sorting office to the rear (demolished). Post offices were not only becoming ever larger but also more widespread; in the year of 1904-5, 69 new offices were erected, with the erection or extension of 142 others begun.[16] Thus, the economies provided by reinforced concrete were of considerable interest to the Office of Works.

How many post offices were constructed in reinforced concrete is unclear, though at least one other trial building is recorded. This survives as a set of contract drawings of 1909 for rebuilding the rear part of the now-demolished Lombard Street office on a tight site in the City of London, using the fearsomely named 'Armoured Concrete-Coignet System'.[17] The Coignet system of reinforcement was a rival to the better known Hennibique system that was used at the King Edward Buildings (the difference was in the way steel bars were connected to the main beams).[18] No finish was specified for the concrete walls overlooking the court, which might have been left exposed. This little-known experimental office was designed by Jasper Wager, the Office of Works architect with responsibility for the London area.

Fig. 10 King Edward Buildings, London, 1907-10, by Henry Tanner. The somewhat ponderous Baroque elevations conceal a daring use of reinforced concrete. [Alan Baxter].

Throughout Henry Tanner's tenure, the Post Office continued to maintain existing Class II Crown Offices and take charge of new ones. The arbitrary separation between these offices and the Class I offices controlled by the Office of Works proved increasingly unsatisfactory from the Post Office's point of view. In 1907 a Select Committee on Post Office Servants concluded that all buildings should be the responsibility of the Post Office. The Government, however, knew better, insisting that the Office of Works ensured 'economy, efficiency and uniformity'. As a sop to the Post Office, it was allowed to appoint an 'Architectural Assistant', Frederick C. R. Palmer, in 1908.[19] Despite the fact that Palmer had once worked for the Office of Works, he was not allowed anywhere near their design programme; instead, he was given the tedious sinecure of advising on the provision of equipment to Class II offices (there were 700 of these in 1907).

EDWARDIAN ECLECTICISM

Tanner remained in charge until 1913, exercising little stylistic control over his ever-growing team of architects. Consequently, post offices of the Edwardian period display the full range of styles associated with the period. One of the leading lights in Tanner's department was Walter Pott (1864–1937), an architect of some originality to whom many of the larger buildings were entrusted. Surviving examples of his work, in a distinguished Baroque style, include Woodhouse Street, Leeds (c.1906), Aberdeen Walk, Scarborough (c.1905), Hull (c.1906), Blackpool (c.1908) and Fitzalan Square, Sheffield (1907–10, **Fig. 11**),[20] the latter with a bold stair tower to the corner.

Fig. 11 Sheffield Post Office, 1907–10, by Walter Pott of HM Office of Works. Full-height channelled rustication imparts power and solidity. [National Archives].

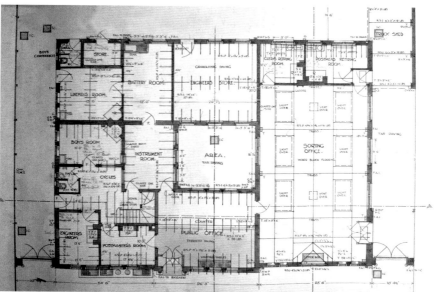

Figs. 12–13 Walton-on-Thames Post Office, Surrey, *c.*1907, by John Rutherford of HM Office of Works. The domestic appearance belies a complex plan. A telegram received in the instrument room could be passed through a hatch to a messenger in the boys' room, who would then make the delivery by bicycle. The upper storey accommodated the telephone switch room, usually staffed entirely by women.

Pott's colleague, John Rutherford, was equally at home in Baroque, Free or Domestic Revival styles, the selection of which seems to have depended partly on local context. For the cathedral city of Canterbury, he designed a Free Gothic post office (*c.*1906). For the old town of Walton-on-Thames, Surrey, a Domestic Revival style was used (*c.*1907), admirably suiting its domestic context. It is rewarding to compare the exterior form of this building with the original ground plan (**Figs. 12–13**).[21] Hiding behind an unassuming half-timbered façade lay a dizzying array of up-to-date facilities, all of which were then standard even in a modest-sized office such as this. The contextual treatment was repeated by other Works architects in locations where the *genius loci* was predominantly domestic in character, such as at East Street, Petworth, Sussex (*c*.1910), where the Neo-Tudor post office is by H. A. Collins of the Office of Works. The theme of sympathy with surroundings continued in a more marked form after the First World War.

POSTSCRIPT: TOWARDS A HOUSE STYLE

It was during the inter-war years that the Post Office achieved its clearest architectural identity. By the time of Tanner's retirement in 1913, the postal network was substantially complete, so that inter-war post offices were mainly built in smaller towns and suburbs. Others required renewal because of the increasing use of the post office, especially the addition of telephone services. The key figure in this period was R. J. Allison, who rose up through the Office of Works to become Chief Architect in 1920. Allison's personal preference for the Neo-Georgian style, which was then becoming popular for public buildings, dominated the output of the post office department in the inter-war years.[22] Modern and yet reassuringly familiar, it became the default house style, deployed on high streets throughout the country (**Fig. 14**). Although the quiet restraint of an inter-war post office made it easy to recognise, it was never taken as far as using the same design in a number of places – post offices were always more tailor-made than Neo-Georgian council housing. The key virtue of inter-war offices is the way they were designed to respect a particular context, which was achieved often through the sensitive use of local materials.

Fig. 14 Clevedon Post Office, Somerset, 1930s, by an unknown HM Office of Works architect. The inter-war Neo-Georgian post offices depended largely on proportion for effect. (Alan Baxter).

Following the Second World War, growing cost pressures made the provision of distinctive new buildings a low priority. There was also insufficient demand for new post offices to justify maintaining a specialist team at the Ministry of Works (as it had become). Consequently, very few new offices were of merit. The fundamental reorganisation of the Post Office began in 1969 when it became a public corporation. Telecommunications was separated in 1981 and privatised in 1984. Meanwhile, the Ministry of Works, which for so long had set its stamp on post office architecture, was itself gradually transformed, ending up in 1972 as the Property Services Agency and finally wound up in 1993.

OVERVIEW

With hindsight, we can appreciate that the period from 1840 to 1914 saw the birth and fruition of the modern Post Office. The introduction of the penny post in 1840 unleashed the full potential of the system, placing such pressure on facilities that specialised post office buildings became essential. Some of these were provided locally but an ever growing number were procured and designed by the Office of Works, firstly under James Williams, whose classical offices bear a strong family resemblance. Williams may have been instrumental in developing the post office plan, though his preferred architectural language perhaps would not have adapted well to the larger offices that were increasingly becoming necessary. Tanner, perhaps realizing that style could not be controlled while Crown II offices by outside architects persisted, concentrated more on technical matters. The requirements that arose from the introduction of the telegraph in 1870, the telephone from the 1880s, and the ever growing volume of post, were accommodated in grand civic monuments that still grace English cities today, though now often converted to other uses.

Just as the public has until recently taken post offices for granted, so historians have tended to overlook them. Certainly, they have not attracted the same attention as other town centre buildings such as banks, shops and civic buildings. Architecturally, they were perhaps never in the vanguard, except during the years when Henry Tanner was experimenting with reinforced concrete. And yet it is remarkable that they were consistently of high quality over the course of a hundred years or so, from 1840. Remarkably, this impressive record is almost entirely due to the anonymous architects of the Office of Works, who proved adept at incorporating ever-changing technical requirements into coherent and attractive architectural compositions.

ACKNOWLEDGEMENT

This essay is based on a report commissioned by English Heritage from Alan Baxter, the research for which was very much a team effort. The findings presented here are thus also the work of Robert Thorne and Anthony Hoyte. Special thanks are due to Julian Osley for kindly sharing his own conclusions with us.

Notes

1. Howard Robinson, *Britain's Post Office: A History of Development from the Beginnings to the Present Day*, London, 1953, p. 25.
2. M. J. Daunton, *Royal Mail: The Post Office Since 1840*, London, 1985, pp. 43-4.
3. Robinson, *Britain's Post Office*, p. 22.
4. British Postal Archive, POST 30/119.
5. Daunton, *Royal Mail,* p. 281; British Postal Archive, POST 30/2339 (papers of the Crawley Committee).
6. C. R. Perry, *The Victorian Post Office: The Growth of a Bureaucracy*, Royal Society Studies in History, no. 64, 1992, p. 5.
7. British Postal Archive, POST 30/2340 (Papers of the Crawley Committee). Evidence of Sir Henry Tanner, 19 July 1912.
8. National Archives, WORK 30/4083, WORK 30/4087.
9. National Archives, WORK 30/3111.
10. Daunton, *Royal Mail,* p. 277.
11. *The Builder*, 12 June 1880, p. 735.
12. National Archives, WORK 30/4903.
13. National Archives, WORK 30/6189.
14. Robinson, *Britain's Post Office*, pp. 206, 218-20.
15. M. H. Port, 'Tanner, Sir Henry (1849-1935)', *Oxford Dictionary of National Biography*, 2004.
16. *The Builder*, 23 September 1905, p. 328.
17. National Archives, WORK 13/337.
18. David Yeomans, *Construction since 1900: Materials*, London, 1997, p. 106.
19. British Postal Archive, POST 30/2339.
20. National Archives, WORK 13/286.
21. National Archives, WORK 13/288.
22. *The Times*, 30 September 1958.

Notes on Authors

Susie Barson is a Senior Architectural Investigator with English Heritage. She is a co-author of the English Heritage publications *A Farewell to Fleet Street* (1988), *London Suburbs* (1999), *The Peabody Estates* (2001), and *Scene/Unseen: London's West End Theatres* (2003). She has also published an essay on Charles Holden's London Underground stations in *The Architecture of British Transport in the Twentieth Century* (Yale, 2004). The history of London's Metropolitan Police Stations was the subject of her post-graduate thesis at the Bartlett School of Architecture (1987).

Geoff Brandwood has particular interests in Victorian and Edwardian architecture. His doctoral thesis has been published as *Bringing them to their Knees: Church-building and Restoration in Leicestershire and Rutland, 1800-1914* (2002). He contributed the churches entries to two 'Pevsners', Leicestershire, and Buckinghamshire, and, in 1997, published a monograph on the great Victorian/Edwardian architect, Temple Moore. He co-authored, with Andrew Davison and Michael Slaughter, *Licensed to Sell: the History and Heritage of the Public House* (2004) for English Heritage. He was chairman of the Victorian Society from 2001 to 2007, and is active in organising events for the society. He is completing a study of the great North-West architectural practice of Sharpe, Paley and Austin for English Heritage.

Andrew Davison works for English Heritage's North West Region, based in Manchester. An archaeologist by training, he also has an MA in building conservation. He has a long-standing interest in the archaeology and architecture of brewing and malting, and has been a member of the Brewery History Society for many years. His eyes were opened to the heritage of the Temperance movement (which was particularly strong in NW England) whilst researching material for the book *Licensed to Sell: the History and Heritage of the Public House* (English Heritage 2004), of which he is the co-author.

Emily Gee has worked in listing at English Heritage since early 2001, and has been Heritage Protection Team Leader responsible for advice to Government on listing, scheduling and registration in London and the South East since 2005. She has an undergraduate degree from Smith College, Massachusetts, an MA in Architectural History from the University of Virginia, and a diploma in Building Conservation from the Architectural Association. She is a member of the IHBC and the Society of Architectural Historians, and is excited to be embarking upon a restoration project of a grade II–listed building, her early Victorian terraced house in Camden Town.

Robert Hradsky is an architectural historian at Alan Baxter, a multi-disciplinary design consultancy based in London. With Robert Thorne and Anthony Hoyte he completed a study on the evolution of purpose-built post offices in England, 1840-1980. This report, commissioned by English Heritage's Research Department, provides an overview of a hitherto neglected building type. He curated exhibitions for SAVE Britain's Heritage (*Triumph, Disaster and Decay: the SAVE survey of Liverpool*, 2009) and Sir John Soane's Museum (*A Passion for Building: the Amateur Architect in England 1650-1850*, 2007, with John Harris) and is Secretary of the Euston Arch Trust. He is currently completing a doctoral thesis on the architectural development of the Inns of Court.

Barbara Lasic studied English literature and history at the Université Denis Diderot, Paris, and history of art at the University of Manchester where, in 2006, she gained a Ph.D on the collecting of eighteenth–century French decorative arts in Britain, 1789-1914. She now works as an assistant curator at the Victoria & Albert Museum. Before joining the V&A, Barbara has held positions at the Wellcome Trust and the National Maritime Museum. More broadly, Barbara has published on the subject of art collecting, the history of taste and country houses collections. Her research interests include the formation of museums, the private and institutional collecting and display of French art in the nineteenth century; and artistic and cultural exchanges between Britain and France.

Adam Menuge is a Senior Architectural Investigator with English Heritage and has a particular interest in the villas and villa landscapes of the English Lake District. He has worked for the National Trust, the Yorkshire Dales National Park, and the Royal Commission on the Historical Monuments of England. He is the author of *Ordinary Landscapes, Special Places: Anfield, Breckfield and the Growth of Liverpool's Suburbs* (2008) and (with Catherine Dewar) of *Berwick-upon-Tweed: Three Places, Two Nations, One Town* (2009). He is a leading exponent of professional training in buildings history and is the principal author of two guidance documents: *Understanding Historic Buildings: A Guide to Good Recording Practice* (2006) and *Understanding Place: Historic Area Assessments – Principles and Practice* (2010).

John Minnis is a Senior Architectural Investigator with English Heritage. He has a particular interests in transport buildings and, with Kathryn Morrison, is currently writing a book, to be published in 2012, on the impact of the motor car on the historic environment of England, which will examine the development of the building types that grew up to serve and accommodate the car. He was the co-author of *Religion and Place in Leeds* (2007) for English Heritage, and the *Pevsner Architectural Guide to Sheffield* (2004). He is also the author of *Southern Country Stations: South Eastern & Chatham Railway* (1985), published by Ian Allan.

Sarah Whittingham is an architectural and garden historian. Her Ph.D was on George Oatley, and her paper on him was published in the Victorian Society's *Powerhouses of Provincial Architecture 1837-1914* (2009). She also wrote *Wills Memorial Building* (2003) on his most significant work, and her biography, *Sir George Oatley: Architect of Bristol*, will be published in 2010. Other books include *The Victorian Fern Craze* (2009) and *Fern Fever: the Story of Pteridomania* (2012), as well as many articles on the subject, including for the National Trust magazine, *Country Life,* and *The English Garden*. She joined the Victorian Society in 1987, was a member of its Education and Publications Committee 1996-2000, the Main Committee 1998-2002, and was a trustee 2002-5.

THE VICTORIAN SOCIETY

The Victorian Society is the champion for Victorian and Edwardian architecture in England and Wales. It was founded in 1958 to make sure that the best Victorian and Edwardian buildings are looked after and enjoyed for many years to come.

It does this by

* speaking out about the value of historic architecture
* running educational events
* advising owners and councils considering changes to listed buildings
* joining with local people to fight for the buildings that matter to them.

Anyone can join. Lectures, walks and tours are organised for members.

The Victorian Society
1 Priory Gardens
London W4 1TT

020 8994 1019

admin@victoriansociety.org.uk
www.victoriansociety.org.uk